Javascript for Beginners

D0972800

Funded by
MISSION COLLEGE
Carl D. Perkins Vocational and Technical Education Act Grant

Javascript for Beginners

Mark Lassoff

LearnToProgram, Inc.
Vernon, Connecticut

LearnToProgram, Incorporated
27 Hartford Turnpike Suite 206
Vernon, CT 06066
contact@learntoprogram.tv
(860) 840-7090

ISBN-13: 978-0-9888429-5-3
ISBN-10: 09888429555

Mark Lassoff, Publisher
Kevin Hernandez, VP Production
Alison Downs, Copy Editor
Alexandria O'Brien, Book Layout
Jimda Mariano, Technical Writer
Karen Doyle, Intern

Dedication

To The Team:

Kevin, our production manager and my partner in crime
Jimda, our technical writer
Alison, our editor
Alex, our designer

A heartfelt thank you!

TABLE OF CONTENTS

About the Author

Mark Lassoff's parents frequently claim that Mark was born to be a programmer. In the mid-eighties when the neighborhood kids were outside playing kickball and throwing snowballs, Mark was hard at work on his Commodore 64 writing games in the BASIC programming language. Computers and programming continued to be a strong interest in college where Mark majored in communication and computer science. Upon completing his college career, Mark worked in the software and web development departments at several large corporations.

In 2001, on a whim, while his contemporaries were conquering the dot-com world, Mark accepted a position - training programmers in a technical training center in Austin, Texas. It was there he fell in love with teaching programming.

Teaching programming has been Mark's passion for the last 10 years. Today Mark is a top technical trainer, traveling the country providing training for software and web developers. Mark's training clients include the Department of Defense, Lockheed Martin, Discover Card Services, and Kaiser Permanente. Mark's clients rate his classes 9.81/10, with consistent perfect scores on participant evaluations.

In addition to traditional classroom training, Mark is a sought after video trainer and host. He has authored and hosted video courses for several publishers, including his own company LearnToProgram.tv, Inc. Mark has authored over 15 online courses and works with students from all 50 states and over 47 countries.

He lives near Hartford, Connecticut in a 150-year-old converted textile mill.

Courses Available from LearnToProgram, Inc.

HTML and CSS for Beginners (with HTML5)
Javascript for Beginners
C# For Beginners
jQuery for Beginners
iOS Development Code Camp
Become a Certified Web Developer
PHP & MySQL for Beginners
iOS Development for Beginners
Objective C for Beginners
C Programming for Beginners
Android Development for Beginners
Creating an MP3 Player with Adobe Flash
AJAX Development
Python for Beginners
CSS Development (with CSS3)
HTML5 Mobile App Development with PhoneGap

Books from LearnToProgram, Inc.

HTML and CSS for Beginners
Creating an MP3 Player with HTML5

CHAPTER 1

HELLO JAVASCRIPT!

CHAPTER OBJECTIVES:

• You will be able to understand client and server side technologies of web applications.
• You will be able to create Javascript within an HTML document.
• You will be able to use the document.write command in Javascript.
• You will understand the different places where you can place Javascript within a document.

1.1 INTRODUCING THE TECHNOLOGIES

Before we begin this course, let us discuss the technologies used in web design and development. There are two types of technologies used within web development. They are client side technologies and server side technologies.

Client Side Technologies: These refer to computer languages that are run and interpreted by the client's browser. Client side technologies include HTML, Javascript and CSS or Cascading Style Sheet Language.

Server Side Technologies: Server side technologies, on the other hand, are a set of applications and software that store the web page code and send it to the user's web browser when requested. These include Java Enterprise Edition, .net, Ruby on Rails, PHP/MySQL, and Perl. These server side technologies usually create HTML code and dispatch that code to the client's browser.

Client and server side technologies often interact with one another to produce the completed web page or application while each performs a distinct role in the process.

In order to succeed in this course, you must already be familiar with HTML. If you are not, it is recommended that you either first take a course on HTML or review an HTML book or manual.

A summary of technologies and languages you will likely encounter while learning Javascript is listed below, briefly outlining each role.

Technology/ Language	Role
HTML	HTML is used to structure web pages. *It is not used to create a design or the look and feel of a website.* HTML markup indicates the purpose of each element—not its page position or appearance. The current standards of HTML are HTML 4.01 and XHTML. HTML5 will be the standard in 2014. HTML is not a programming language, but is a markup language that consists of tags, attributes and content.
CSS	CSS was derived to add a design component to HTML. It allows typography control, color control, layout and design features like margins, padding and borders.
Javascript	Javascript is a client side technology that adds interactivity to web pages. Javascript code can be used to validate user input, create dropdown effects, switch CSS styles dynamically and even make complex calculations. Javascript has become more important lately as more processing moves from the server side to the client side. Client side processing is more efficient, leads to a better user experience and is event based. Javascript is not compiled, but is interpreted by the browser.
AJAX	AJAX (Asynchronous Javascript and XML) is an application of Javascript that allows communication between the client and server to take place "behind the scenes." This results in a smoother, more desktop-like interface for web applications.

TABLE 1 - 1

QUESTIONS FOR REVIEW

1. Is Javascript run on client side or server side?
   a. Server side.
   b. Client side.
   c. Both.
   d. Neither.

2. Javascript is defined as:
   a. A programming language that allows you to play games and run applications on the web.
   b. A language that allows you to change the style of HTML.
   c. A scripting language used to add interactivity to web pages.
   d. A language that allows you to create basic web pages.

1.2 HELLO WORLD IN JAVASCRIPT

Let's go ahead and create your first Javascript program. You will need two items to create your first Javascript. First you need a web browser. It is highly recommended that you use multiple web browsers in order to make sure your program works in different browsers. You also need a text editor, which is usually preinstalled in your computer. However, you can also use one of the more sophisticated text editors, such as ActiveState's Komodo Edit or Notepad++. The one program you should not use is a word processor, as they insert formatting that a web browser will not understand.

Komodo Edit

Notepad++

You will write your first Javascript program within a basic HTML document. Create a document structure with a head and a body and title your document "First Javascript".

```
<html>
<head>
<title>First Javascript</title>
</head>
<body>
</body>
</html>
```

Then insert a script tag in the body to tell your browser that you will be using Javascript. Set the script language attribute to Javascript and assign the attribute type to "text/javascript". The complete script tag for including Javascript in HTML is:

<script>

```
<script language="javascript" type="text/
javascript">
```

Next we are going to use the **document.write** command in Javascript. This basic command will output the specified text on the web page. If you are displaying text, enclose your text output in parentheses, followed by quotation marks. This is how the document.write command is written:

```
document.write("Hello World from
Javascript");
```

It's a good idea to end your Javascript commands with a semi-colon. Many programming languages require a semi-colon at the end of each command. In Javascript, the semi-colon is optional, but, even so, it is a good idea to use it to keep your code organized and develop best practices for writing programming code.

You may also want to add comments to your code. Comments are an extremely useful way of keeping your code organized and neat. Imagine the inconvenience when you need to revise your code but can't remember how your code was structured. You will definitely have to take the time to review and figure out your code before you can edit it. Comments help you quickly and efficiently label and review your code. In Javascript, you put comments in your code by preceding your line with //. An example of a comment would be:

```
//This is a comment in Javascript
```

Javascript also allows the developer to write multiline comments. Within the browser, the Javascript interpreter ignores any content between the opening multiline comment symbol and the closing symbol. An example of a multiline comment appears below:

```
/*
    This is an example of a multiline
comment
    Mark Lassoff
    Spring, 2013
*/
```

Within document.write() commands, you may embed HTML tags which change the way your text is formatted. In order to use tags, you must place them within your quotation marks. For example, if you want your text to appear bold, you use a strong tag. Your code to display bold text should look like this:

```
document.write("<strong>Hello World from
Javascript</strong>");
```

> Make sure you close the tag within the quotation marks.

There is a useful tag called the break **
** tag, which is used to display your text or your output on separate lines. The break <br/> tag must be placed within the quotation marks. Also, your script tag must be closed at the end of the Javascript code. The program may not run if you fail to close the script tag.

CODE LISTING: FIRST JAVASCRIPT

```
<!DOCTYPE HTML PUBLIC "-//W3C//DTD HTML
4.01//EN"
    "http://www.w3.org/TR/html4/strict.dtd"
>
<html>
    <head>
        <title>First Javascript</title>
    </head>
    <body>
        <script language="javascript"
type="text/javascript">

    //Output to the browser
    document.write("<strong>Hello World
from Javascript</strong>");
    document.write("<br/>This is my first
Javascript program!");
        </script>
    </body>
</html>
```

First Javascript

Hello World from Javascript
This is my first Javascript program!

Here is the Javascript output on the browser. Observe how the upper text is displayed as bold and the <br/> tag is used to create a break between the two lines. If there was no break tag, the two sentences would appear on the same line.

FIGURE 1 - 1

QUESTIONS FOR REVIEW

1. What two items do you need to begin programming in Javascript?
   a. A computer and headphones.
   b. A mouse and a microphone.
   c. Microsoft Office and a keyboard.
   d. A web browser and a text editor.

2. Which command in Javascript outputs text to the browser?
   a. document.text
   b. document.write()
   c. document.output
   d. document.go

3. Which HTML tag can you use within the Javascript document.write() command to separate lines in the browser?
   a.
   b. <b>
   c. <strong>
   d. <em>

Create a Javascript application which produces the output below when viewed in the browser. You must create your output using Javascript commands, not HTML:

First Javascript

Hello World from Javascript
This is my first Javascript program. Hurray!

FIGURE 1 - 2

LAB SOLUTION

```
<!DOCTYPE HTML PUBLIC "-//W3C//DTD HTML
4.01//EN"
    "http://www.w3.org/TR/html4/strict.dtd"
>
<html lang="en">
<head>
    <title>First Javascript</title>
</head>
<body>
    <script language="javascript"
type="text/javascript">
        document.write("Hello World from
Javascript <br/>");
        document.write("<strong>This is
my first Javascript program.</strong>
Hurray!");
    </script>
</body>
</html>
```

1.3 WHERE TO PUT JAVASCRIPT

In the previous section, we created Javascript code and placed it in the body of the HTML document. Javascript can be placed in the head of the document, or as an external file called from the HTML code as well. In this chapter, we will review all three places where you can put your Javascript code.

We have already placed Javascript in the body using the script tag. Placing the script tag in the head of the document works just the same.

Typically though, Javascript best directs output to the browser when it is in the body of the document. The head usually contains functions, which are lines of Javascript that are executed later when called upon in the document. We'll discuss how to use functions later in the book, but for now we are just going to use one as an example of how to place Javascript code in the head of the document.

Functions are implemented through the identifier **function**, followed by the name of the function and two parentheses. Function is coded as:

```
function sayBye()
{
document.write("Buh Bye");
}
```

The actual code that the function executes is found inside the curly brackets following the name of the function. In the above example, we used the **document.write()** command to create the simple output "Buh Bye".

The **function** by itself will not generate the expected output to the browser. To display the text, we need to call our function. To call the function, we need to use the function name within a set of script tags. We have placed these script tags in the document body:

```
<body>
    <script language="javascript"
type="text/javascript">
sayBye();
</script>
</body>
```

Let us include the previous body element in a complete code listing that will have two functions in its code. Refer to the following code listing:

CODE LISTING: WHERE TO PUT JAVASCRIPT

```
<!DOCTYPE HTML PUBLIC "-//W3C//DTD HTML
4.01//EN"
    "http://www.w3.org/TR/html4/strict.dtd"
>
<html>
    <head>
        <title>First Javascript</title>
        <script language="javascript"
type="text/javascript">
            function sayBandName()
            {
                document.write("Journey
rules!<br/>");
            }
            function sayBye()
            {
                document.write("Buh Bye!");
            }
        </script>
    </head>
    <body>
        <script language="javascript"
type="text/javascript">
            //Output to the browser
            document.write("<strong>Hello World
from Javascript.</strong>");
            document.write("<br/>This is my
first Javascript program!<br/>");
        sayBandName();
        sayBye();
        </script>
    </body>
</html>
```

Two functions are now included in this example. Two separate document. write() commands were also included here. The two functions were placed in the head <script> element while the function calls were placed right before the ending </body> tag.

The previous code will display the following output when viewed in the browser:

● ○ ○	First Javascript

Hello World from Javascript.
This is my first Javascript program!
Journey rules!
Buh Bye!

FIGURE 1 - 3

The other method of inserting Javascript in your HTML document is by including an external Javascript document in the script tag, as shown below:

```
<script language="javascript" type="type/
javascript"
```

And the source attribute link:

```
src="attached.js"></script>
```

which points to the Javascript (.js) file attachment called *attached.js*.

Let's create an external Javascript document. Create a new HTML document and save it under the file name *JavascriptExternal.html*. Inside that document, type the following code. This will implement the .js attachment.

CODE LISTING: ATTACHED JAVASCRIPT

```
<!DOCTYPE HTML PUBLIC "-//W3C//DTD HTML
4.01//EN"
    "http://www.w3.org/TR/html4/strict.dtd" >
```

```
<html>
    <head>
        <title>Attached</title>
    </head>
    <body>
        <script language="javascript"
                    type="text/javascript"
                    src="attached.js">
        </script>
    </body>
</html>
```

In the previous code, you are telling the script tag to load the Javascript file *attached.js* and whatever instructions the external Javascript file has will be executed in the HTML.

The second task is constructing the external Javascript file, *attached.js*. Any Javascript command can be placed inside that document.

For our example, we will do a simple activity that uses the document. write command. Notice in the code within the attached Javascript file that you do not need any HTML or script tags. This file should just contain the Javascript commands.

Create a new blank text document. Save the file and name it *attached.js*. Inside the document, type the following code and then save.

CODE LISTING: ATTACHED JAVASCRIPT FILE

```
document.write("This came from the attached
Javascript file!<br/>");
document.write("Some think that attaching
Javascript is the best way to use it with
HTML!");
```

View your HTML file in a browser and make sure that it displays the text contained in the document.write() commands in the external Javascript file. The source attribute of the <script> tag is responsible for calling the external file *attached.js*. Following is the output when the whole code listing is run:

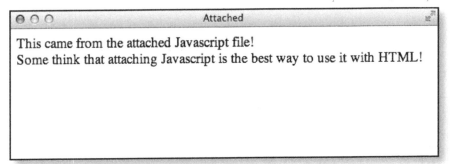

FIGURE 1 - 4

In many situations it is definitely best to attach the Javascript rather than embedding it in your HTML. Attaching your Javascript in an external file makes maintenance of your application easier because you don't have to dig through your HTML to find your Javascript code. Additionally, externalizing your Javascript promotes reuse of the Javascript code in other applications.

QUESTIONS FOR REVIEW

1. Traditionally, which Javascript component is found in the head of the document?
   a. An output.
   b. A comment.
   c. A function.
   d. Javascript cannot be put into the head.

2. If you wanted to create a Javascript function called sayGo, how would you introduce it in the code?
   a. function sayGo()   c. sayGo();
   b. sayGo;   d. function sayGo;

3. Which attribute do you use to load an external Javascript file?
   a. src=***.js
   b. external=***.js
   c. source=***.js
   d. Javascript cannot be placed externally.

4. Which of the following is not a place you can put Javascript?
   a. The head of the document.   c. The body of the document.
   b. External file.   d. The foot of the document.

1) Create a Javascript code that will display the following output:

⊖ ○ ○   Javascript: Unordered list and style

Mark Lassoff
Plainview, NY

- Journey
- REO Speedwagon
- Styx
- Heart

FIGURE 1 - 5

2) Add code that will display on the first line your name in italics and, on the second line, the city where you were born.

3) Starting on the third line, add code to display four unordered list items of your choice, for example, your four favorite bands.

CHAPTER 1 LAB SOLUTION

```html
<!DOCTYPE HTML PUBLIC "-//W3C//DTD HTML
4.01//EN"
    "http://www.w3.org/TR/html4/strict.dtd"
>
<html>
    <head>
     <title>Javascript: Unordered list and
style
     </title>
    </head>

    <body>
        <script language="javascript"
            type="text/javascript"
            src="/****/ch1LabSol.js">
        </script>
    <ul>
        <li>Journey</li>
        <li>REO Speedwagon</li>
        <li>Styx</li>
        <li>Heart</li>
    </ul>

    </body>
</html>
```

Replace the bold text with your own file's pathname.

This is the solution for the .js attachment. The complete file name is *chLabSol.js*:

```javascript
document.write("<em>Mark Lassoff</
em><br/>");
document.write("Plainview, NY");
```

Chapter 1 Summary

In this chapter we discussed the nature of client and server side technologies that are employed with Javascript and how each functions and differs from one another. You learned the difference between client side and server side web technologies. We also discussed why Javascript is extremely useful for web developers.

You also learned how to create your first Javascript program using the document.write() command in Javascript to output a message to the screen.

You learned the various places you can insert your Javascript code. First, you may place Javascript in the body of the document, second, in the HTML <head> element, and lastly Javascript may be placed in an external document.

You also learned that the Javascript function is best used in the head of HTML documents.

In the next chapter, we will be discussing how to use variables. Variables are one of the most important elements of any programming language. You will learn how to create and manipulate Javascript variables.

CHAPTER 2

STORING INFORMATION
IN VARIABLES

CHAPTER OBJECTIVES:

• You will learn how to declare and initialize variables.
• You will be able to change the values of variables.
• You will learn how to use arithmetic operators.
• You will learn how to concatenate strings and variables.

2.1 LEARNING TO USE VARIABLES

In this chapter we are going to discuss variables. Variables are important elements of any programming language, and Javascript is no exception.

 Variables are memory allocations used to hold values. They are called variables because their value may vary over time throughout the execution of the program.

You can use variables to hold text values (also known as alphabetic or string values) such as a person's name, company name or any other text content in your program. Variables may also hold numerical values.

To show you how variables are used, let's start with an HTML document page. For this example, we will use an HTML 4.01 document. To insert Javascript, a script tag is used with attributes set as follows:

```
<script language="javascript" type="text/
javascript">
```

All Javascript commands must be placed within the script element. The first Javascript element that must be identified is the variable to be used. We need to name the variable and declare it.

When you declare a variable in Javascript, you use the **var** statement followed by the name of the variable. It is ideal that the name of the variable is something that describes what the variable represents. The variable name can be any alphanumeric set of characters, and should be treated as case sensitive. No punctuation marks or special characters are allowed, except for underscore.

An example of a variable declaration is:

```
var userName;
```

It's not required to use the var statement when declaring a variable in Javascript, however, it is a good idea always to do so. Consistently using var when declaring variables avoids difficulties with variable scope.

We'll be discussing variable scope later in the course, but the short explanation is that there are variables that are only used within a certain segment of your program, such as a function. Variables can be declared so that their value is only retrievable within that scope.

Now that we have declared our variable, we can assign it a value. This is called **variable assignment**. When we set the initial value of the variable, it is known as **initialization**. Once you have declared your variable, you no longer need to use the var statement. All you need is the name of the variable followed by the equal sign and the value of the variable. In this example, our variable initialization is:

```
userName="Mark Lassoff";
```

The value assigned in the above example is a string, also known as text, which is why it was enclosed with quotes. If you are assigning a numerical value to a variable, you do not need to enclose the value with quotes. For example:

```
age = 39;
```

A shortcut method for simultaneously declaring and initializing variables is to combine declaration and initialization on the same line. This is a more efficient way of initializing and declaring a variable. Declaring and initializing a variable concurrently is as follows:

```
var userName="Mark Lassoff";
```

We can now display the variable's value. To display the value of the variable you can use the *document.write()* command, followed by the name of the variable in parentheses. The command syntax is:

```
document.write(userName);
```

When you want to display the variable's value, you do not need to put quotes around the variable name (like you would if you were outputting text). Instead you simply write the variable name in the parentheses. If it is the actual string value you want to print, then surrounding the string value with quotes is a must. For example:

```
document.write ("Austin, Texas");
```

> This will display Austin, Texas.

We can also change the value of a variable during the program's execution. Suppose you have displayed the first value assigned to your variable. You then assign another value to the same variable name and then have it displayed. The second value assigned to *userName* replaces the initial value.

So far, we have been assigning values to our variable with the equal sign. However, the equal sign does not mean "equal to" in the context of Javascript. In Javascript, the equal sign is known as the **assignment operator**. The assignment operator merely assigns a value to the variable.

We will discuss more operators and their functions in greater detail later on. The way we read the variable initialization in the previous example is that the variable *userName* was assigned the value Mark Lassoff. The value being in quotes indicates it as a string value.

When a number is assigned as the value of a variable, it is referred to as a **numeric variable**. This is an example of declaring and assigning a numeric variable:

```
var userAge= 37;
```

In the next section, we will use numeric variables to perform some arithmetic operations.

The complete example code listing for the above discussion is presented here, followed by a screenshot of the expected output when viewed in the browser.

CODE LISTING: DECLARING AND ASSIGNING VARIABLES

```
<!DOCTYPE HTML PUBLIC "-//W3C//DTD HTML
4.01//EN"
    "http://www.w3.org/TR/html4/strict.dtd"
>
<html lang="en">
<head>
    <title></title>
</head>
<body>
    <script language="javascript"
            type="text/javascript">

        //var userName="Mark Lassoff";

        var userName;
//Variable Declaration
        userName="Mark Lassoff";
//Variables Initialization
        document.write(userName);
//No quotes:  Output value of variables
        userName="Brett Lassoff";
// = Known as the assignment operator
        document.write("<br/>");
        document.write(userName);
        document.write("<br/>");
        var userAge = 37;
//Combined initialization/declaration
        document.write(userAge);

    </script>
</body>
</html>
```

This is how the output appears in the browser. Notice how the names and age were displayed on separate lines. This was made possible by using the break *
* tags, along with the *document.write()* command.

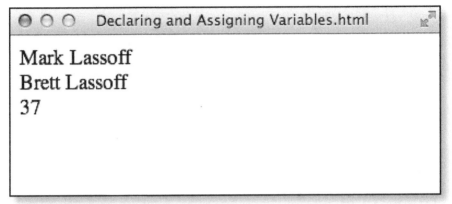

FIGURE 2 - 1

QUESTIONS FOR REVIEW

1. In Javascript, what statement do you use to declare a variable?
   - a. variable
   - b. declare
   - c. var
   - d. dar

2. What happens if you don't put quotes around a variable's string assigned value?
   - a. The script outputs the value of the variable.
   - b. You get an HTML error.
   - c. The script will not assign the variable correctly.
   - d. Nothing will happen.

3. Which of the following is known as the assignment operator in Javascript?
   - a. The + sign
   - b. The = sign
   - c. The – sign
   - d. The @ sign

4. Which is an example of combined initialization/declaration?
   - a. var Size
   - b. Size = 0
   - c. var Size; Size = 0;
   - d. var Size = 0;

5. Why is it important to use the var statement every time you declare a variable?
    a. You will have trouble with variable scope if you don't.
    b. Variables won't work without being declared.
    c. It's confusing without it.
    d. You shouldn't use it.

LAB ACTIVITY

1) Create a Javascript code that will display the following output:

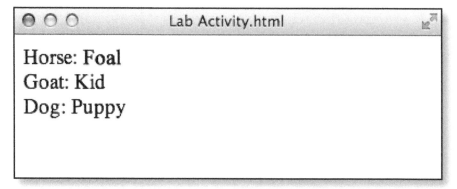

FIGURE 2 - 2

2) The program must have two variables. The first variable will hold the values for the adult animals, *adultAnimalName*, while the second variable will hold the values for the young animal, *youngAnimalName*.

3) Assign one value to each of the variables. Have these two variable values displayed using *document.write()*.

4) Use the following values for your program:

adultAnimalName	youngAnimalName
Horse	Foal
Goat	Kid
Dog	Puppy

TABLE 1 - 1

LAB ACTIVITY SOLUTION: CODE LISTING

```
<!DOCTYPE HTML PUBLIC "-//W3C//DTD HTML
4.01//EN"
"http://www.w3.org/TR/html4/strict.dtd"
    >
<html lang="en">
<head>
    <title></title>
</head>
<body>
    <script language="javascript"
type="text/javascript">
        var adultAnimalName;
        var youngAnimalName;

        adultAnimalName = "Horse";
        youngAnimalName = "Foal";

        document.write(adultAnimalName);
    document.write(": ");
        document.write(youngAnimalName);
        document.write("<br/>");

        adultAnimalName = "Goat";
        youngAnimalName = "Kid";

        document.write(adultAnimalName);
    document.write(": ");
        document.write(youngAnimalName);
        document.write("<br/>");

        adultAnimalName = "Dog";
        youngAnimalName = "Puppy";

        document.write(adultAnimalName);
    document.write(": ");
```

```
            document.write(youngAnimalName);
            document.write("<br/>");

        </script>
    </body>
    </html>
```

2.2 VARIABLE OPERATORS

In this section we are going to discuss variable operators. Once again, start with an HTML 4.01 file, and make sure you include a <script> tag to indicate to the browser that we are using Javascript. First, we need to declare two variables as *operandOne* and *operandTwo*. These two variables will be assigned the values 125 and 15.371, respectively.

Note that they are two distinct value types. The variable *operandOne* holds the **integer number** 125, while the variable *operandTwo* contains the **floating point number** 15.371. A floating point number is capable of holding numbers with decimal points.

```
operandOne = 125;
operandTwo = 15.371;
```

In other programming languages, you would normally have to declare the specific variable type—you have to tell the program if you are using an integer or a floating point number. However, Javascript automatically understands what variable type you are creating the moment you assign its value. There is no need to explicitly specify which type of variable you are using.

With our variables defined and initialized, we can have them displayed as output using the *document.write()* command. Since you are instructing that the program's output be whatever the variable contains, you do not need quotation marks. Let us display the two values on two different lines. The code should be written as follows:

```
document.write (operandOne);
document.write ("<br/>");
document.write (operandTwo);
```

We can also perform arithmetic operations with our variables. To add the two numbers together, we use the addition operator "+". If we want the sum of the two variables displayed, then our code should be:

```
document.write("The sum is " + (operandOne
+ operandTwo))
```

The addition operator is used twice in this example. The plus (+) sign has two purposes in Javascript—it can be used as a **string concatenation operator,** and also as an **addition operator**. When we write *operandOne + operandTwo*, we are using it to add the two variables.

Concatenation, on the other hand, is also an important operation in any programming language. In Javascript, concatenation joins two strings or values together. In the context of this example, we are concatenating (placing next to each other) the string value "The sum is" to the sum of the two variables. The addition operation is placed within its own parentheses so the program understands that it is a separate operation from the concatenation.

Here is a list of the variable operators you can use and how they function:

Operator	Symbol	Function
Addition	+	Adds variables together and concatenates strings and other values.
Subtraction	-	Subtracts the value of one variable from another.
Multiplication	*	Multiplies variables.
Division	/	Divides one variable from another.
Modulus	%	Outputs the remainder of the division operation.
Increment	++	Adds one to the value of the variable.
Decrement	--	Subtracts one from the value of the variable.

TABLE 2 - 2

The increment and decrement operators function by increasing and decreasing, respectively, the value of the variable by one.

There are two ways to use the increment and decrement operators. When the operator is placed after the variable, it is called a **postfix operator**. This means that the mathematical expression is evaluated and then the increment takes place.

The second method is when the operator is placed before the variable; it is called a **prefix operator**. In this situation, the increment takes place first, after which the mathematical operation is performed. Prefix and postfix for mathematical operators do not have much relevance when you simply want to display the output. Significance between the prefix and postfix will be important in the discussion of loops later in the course.

The following code listing provides examples on how each variable operator is used.

CODE LISTING: VARIABLE OPERATORS

```
<!DOCTYPE HTML PUBLIC "-//W3C//DTD HTML
4.01//EN"
    "http://www.w3.org/TR/html4/strict.dtd"
    >
<html lang="en">
<head>
    <title></title>
</head>
<body>
    <script language="javascript"
type="text/javascript">
        var operandOne;
        var operandTwo;
        operandOne = 125;        //Integer
        operandTwo = 15.371;     //Floating
Point Number

        document.write(operandOne);
        document.write("<br/>");
        document.write(operandTwo);
        document.write("<br/>");
        document.write("Addition " +
(operandOne + operandTwo));
        document.write("<br/>");
        document.write("Subtraction " +
(operandOne - operandTwo));
        document.write("<br/>");
        document.write("Multiplication " +
(operandOne * operandTwo));
        document.write("<br/>");
```

```javascript
        document.write("Division " +
(operandOne/operandTwo));
        document.write("<br/>");
        document.write("10 % 3 " + (10 %
3));
        document.write("<br/>");
        document.write("11 % 3 " + (11 %
3));
        operandOne++;      //Increment
Operator Add One to the variable;
        operandTwo--;      //Decrementing
One from the variable
        document.write("<br/>");
        document.write(operandOne);
        document.write("<br/>");
        document.write(operandTwo);
        /*
            variable++    <--- PostFix
Increment Operator
            ++variable    <--- PreFix
Increment Operator

            PostFix- The rest of the
mathematical expression is evaluated and
then
            the increment takes place

            PreFix-  The increment takes
place and then the rest of the expression
            is evaluated
        */
        var teamCity;
        var teamName;

        teamCity ="New York";
        teamName= "Yankees";
        var fullTeamInfo = teamCity + " " +
teamName;
```

```
        document.write("<br/>");
        document.write(fullTeamInfo);
    </script>
</body>
</html>
```

In order to better understand how concatenation works, an example of concatenating two string variables and outputting them is demonstrated within the previous code. We have created a new variable called *fullTeamInfo* and concatenated the two variables *teamCity* and *teamName*. We also concatenated a space within the quotation marks so the two variable strings are spaced properly. The output "New York Yankees" is the result.

This is a screenshot of the output shown in the browser. Here all possible use of concatenation is shown; all four mathematical operations are also demonstrated including the modulus operator.

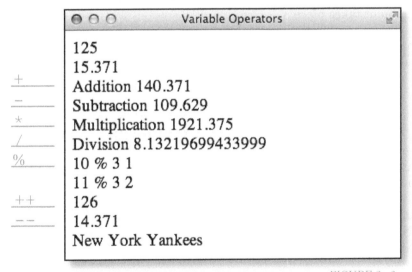

FIGURE 2 - 3

QUESTIONS FOR REVIEW

1. What does the "+" symbol mean when you place it next to a numerical variable?

a. Add the values together.
b. Take away the values.
c. Concatenate the values.
d. Divide the values.

2. What does the "+" symbol mean when you place it between two string values?
   a. Add the values together.
   b. Take away the values.
   c. Concatenate the values.
   d. Divide the values.

3. What does the % operator do?
   a. Gives you the sum of division.
   b. Gives you the remainder after division.
   c. Gives you the multiplication sum.
   d. Gives you the subtraction sum.

4. Which is the increment operator?
   a. –   c. ++
   b. *   d. #

5. How does a prefix increment operator function?
   a. It adds one to the variable.
   b. The rest of the mathematical expression is evaluated and the increment takes place.
   c. It subtracts one from the variable.
   d. The increment takes place and then the rest of the expression is evaluated.

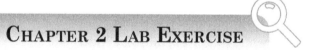

CHAPTER 2 LAB EXERCISE

1) Create an HTML 4.01 document. In the document body, add script tags with the appropriate attributes to add Javascript code.

2) Declare the following variables (but do not initialize yet):
   firstName
   lastName
   age
   city
   favoriteFood

3) Initialize the variables with information about you. (Your first name, last name, age, etc.)

4) Create a variable called *operand1* and use combined initialization and assignment to assign it an initial value of 1555.

5) Create a variable called *operand2* and use combined initialization and assignment to assign it an initial value of **96.255**.

6) Demonstrate your knowledge of the mathematical operators with *operand1* and *operand2* by adding, subtracting, multiplying, and dividing the two values. Format your output as follows:

1555 + 96.255 = 1651.255

The line of code that would produce this output is:

```
document.write(operand1 + " + " + operand2
+ " = " + (operand1+operand2));
```

7) Demonstrate the use of increment operator with *operand1* and decrement operators with *operand2*. Display the results.

CHAPTER 2 LAB EXERCISE SOLUTION

This is how the output will look when viewed in the browser:

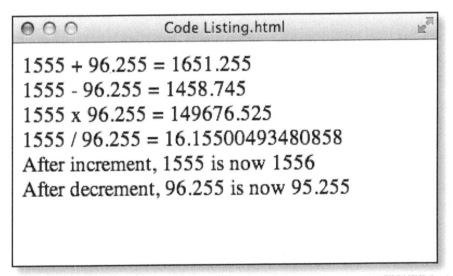

FIGURE 2 - 4

```
<!DOCTYPE HTML PUBLIC "-//W3C//DTD HTML 4.01//EN"
    "http://www.w3.org/TR/html4/strict.dtd"
    >
<html lang="en">
<head>
    <title></title>
</head>
<body>
    <script language="javascript"
type="text/javascript">

        var firstName;
        var lastName;
        var age;
        var city;
        var favoriteFood;

        firstName = "Bob";
        lastName = "Smith";
        age = 45;
        city = "Boston";
        favoriteFood = "Continental";

        var operand1 = 1555;
        var operand2 = 96.255;

        document.write(operand1 +"
+ "+operand2 + " = " + (operand1 +
operand2));
        document.write("<br/>");
        document.write(operand1 +"
- "+operand2 + " = " + (operand1 -
operand2));
        document.write("<br/>");
```

```
        document.write(operand1 +"
x "+operand2 + " = " + (operand1 *
operand2));
        document.write("<br/>");
        document.write(operand1 +"
/ "+operand2 + " = " + (operand1 /
operand2));
        document.write("<br/>");

        document.write("After increment, "
+ operand1 + " is now ");
        operand1++;
        document.write(operand1);
        document.write("<br/>");

        document.write("After decrement, "
+ operand2 + " is now ");
        operand2--;
        document.write(operand2);
        document.write("<br/>");

        /* Since there were no instructions
to display the values of the first five
variables that were asked to be declared
and assigned, they will not be seen in the
output */
        </script>
</body>
</html>
```

CHAPTER 2 SUMMARY

In this chapter we learned about variables, their declaration, initialization, and combined initialization/declaration. You also learned how to output variables.

We also discussed operators, which included the assignment operator and arithmetic operators. You learned that the plus sign (+) can be used as an addition operator or concatenation operator and also learned how to concatenate strings and variables.

In the next chapter we will be discussing conditionals. Conditionals are an extremely important component to any programming language. You will learn both simple and complex conditionals.

CHAPTER 3

CONDITIONAL STATEMENTS

CHAPTER OBJECTIVES:

- You will understand how conditional statements work.
- You will be able to use if-statements.
- You will be able to implement if-else-if statements.
- You will be able to create switch-case-break statements.

3.1 SIMPLE CONDITIONALS

As you develop more complex Javascript programs, it will become important that your programs are able to make decisions. These decisions are expressed as conditionals. In this chapter, we are going to create programs with conditionals.

Conditional statements let your program make some basic criteria-based decisions and do what is called branching. Conditional statements simply allow the program to run certain code testing whether a condition is either true or false and react accordingly.

Let's start with the simplest conditionals set, the **if**-statement.

The if conditional works this way: if the condition is true, the program will run a selected code block; if the condition is false, the code is not executed.

> **Conditional Statments:**
> - If true, the select code will run.
> - If false, the select code will NOT run.

Create a basic HTML document and include the <script> tags. Next, within the script tags, declare a variable named *age* and initialize its value to 18.

We're going to write a short Javascript program that can determine whether someone is eligible to vote. In the US, the voting age is 18. We're going to test the variable age for voting eligibility. The condition should be: if the age is equal to 18 or above, the program will execute code to display the output "You can vote". If the age is less than 18, the code will not be executed. The basic document structure with the script tags should look like this:

```
<html>
   <head>
      <title>Can You Vote?</title>
   </head>
<body>
   <script language=" javascript"
type="text/javascript">
   var age = 19;
   </script>
</body>
</html>
```

Now that we've set up our code, we need to discuss comparison operators and how they work in conjunction with the if-statement

This is how the if-statement condition is written:

```
if (age >= 18)
```

In the above if-statement, the >= symbols found between "age" and "18" is what we call the **comparison operator**. It is read as "greater than or equal to". We used the "greater than or equal to" comparison operator to test the variable *age* if it is greater than or equal to 18 (years old, that is). When the if-statement is evaluated by the Javascript interpreter it will be interpreted as TRUE or FALSE. If it is TRUE, then we want the string "You can vote" to be displayed.

>=

Below is the code set that will display the message "You can vote" followed by a line break. This is executed when the condition evaluates to a TRUE value.

```
if(age>=18)
   {
   document.write("You can vote<br/>");
   }
```

The complete code listing appears as follows:

CODE LISTING: COMPARISON OPERATOR ">="

```
<!DOCTYPE html>
<html>
    <head>
        <title>If Condition</title>
    </head>
<body>
    <script language="javascript"
type="text/javascript">
var age = 18;
if(age>=18)
{
document.write("You can vote.<br/>");
}
</script>
</body>
</html>
```

The output should look like this when viewed in the browser:

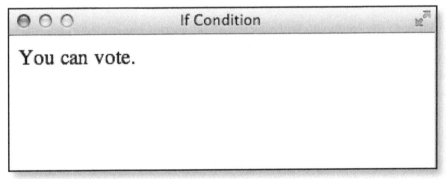

FIGURE 3 - 1

There are several other comparison operators in Javascript. It is important to know how these comparison operators evaluate conditional expressions, as each addresses a unique circumstance.

Here is a list of comparison operators and their functions.

Comparison Operator	Function
==	Equal to
===	Equal to value and type
>	Greater than
<	Less than
>=	Greater than or equal to
<=	Less than or equal to
!=	Not equal to

TABLE 3 - 1

Let's examine another if-statement with a different comparison operator. This time, let us practice with "==", called "equal to", as the comparison operator.

> By the way—it's a common mistake to confuse the assignment operator "=" with the comparison equality operator "==". When I teach classroom Javascript courses in front of live students, it is one of the most common errors I see them make on the lab assignments. Be careful!

Adding to the confusion is the fact that Javascript has an "===" operator that means equal in value and type. I've never actually used this operator in live production Javascript code that I have written; however, it does have a distinct meaning. Examine the following:

```
"1" == 1    TRUE
"1" === 1   FALSE
```

Essentially, the first statement above is evaluated as TRUE because both sides of the statement have the same value: 1. The "==" operator tests value only. You will note that the first 1 is a string because it is encased in quotes. The second 1 is a pure number value. Since "===" tests for type and equality, the second statement is evaluated as FALSE since the type is not the same. Now we'll take a look at our equality conditional operator in action. Declare a variable called *name* whose value is equal to "Mark". Let the condition be: when the variable is equal to the value "Mark", the string "You are the course instructor." would be displayed on the second line. The code to perform the routine is:

```
var name="Mark"

if (name=="Mark")
    {
        document.write("You are the course
instructor")
    }
```

The complete code listing is:

CODE LISTING: COMPARISON OPERATOR "=="

```
<!DOCTYPE HTML PUBLIC "-//W3C//DTD HTML
4.01//EN"
    "http://www.w3.org/TR/html4/strict.dtd"
>
<html lang="en">
<head>
    <title>Simple Condition, Comparison
Operators</title>
</head>
<body>
    <script>
        var name = "Mark";
            if (name =="Mark")
            {document.write("You are the
course instructor.");
            }
    </script>
</body>
</html>
```

The output should look like this when viewed in the browser:

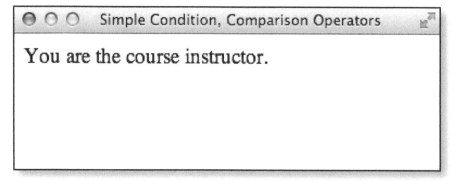

FIGURE 3 - 2

If you change the assigned value of *name* to a string value other than "Mark", the browser will display a blank page. This is because a different assigned value will cause the conditional statement to be evaluated as FALSE, preventing the subsequent code block from being executed.

The remaining comparison operators function similarly. We'll examine the remaining comparison operators so you can see an example of how each is used. Here is the complete code for the activity:

CODE LISTING: COMPARISON OPERATORS

```
<!DOCTYPE HTML PUBLIC "-//W3C//DTD HTML
4.01//EN"
    "http://www.w3.org/TR/html4/strict.dtd"
    >
<html lang="en">
<head>
    <title>Simple Conditionals, Comparison
Operators</title>
</head>
<body>
    <script>
        var name="Mark";
            if (name == "Mark")  //equal to
            {
```

```javascript
document.write("You are the course
instructor. <br/>");
        }

    var course = "Javascript";
if (course === "Javascript")
//equal to value and type
        {
document.write("This course is called
Javascript. <br/>");
        }

    var temperature=39;
if (temperature > 37.5)        //greater than
        {
document.write("You've got fever!<br/>");
        }

    var level=0;
        if(level < 1)    //less than
        {
document.write("That is below the minimum
level.<br/>");
        }
    var age=18;
        if (age >= 18)
//greater than or equal to
        {
document.write("You can vote.<br/>");
        }
    var age=17;
        if (age <= 17)
//less than or equal to
        {
document.write("You are still below legal
age.<br/>");
        }
    var value=0;
```

```
            if (value != 1) //not equal to
            {
document.write("The values are not
equal.<br/>");
            }
    </script>
</body>
</html>
```

The output of the above code when viewed in the browser will look like this:

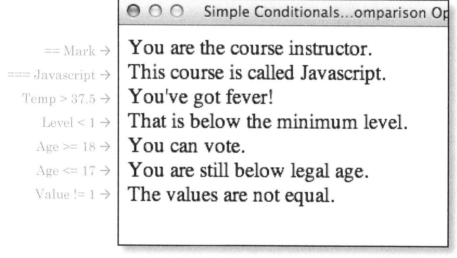

FIGURE 3 - 3

More than one condition can also be associated with the if-statement. When you have multiple conditions within an if-statement, the statement is known as a **complex conditional**. There are two logical comparison operators that can be used to join conditions together.

The first logical comparison operator is the double ampersand - **&&** which evaluates a logical AND comparison. It tests whether the value of the two conditions are both true. If they are, then the if-statement is evaluated as TRUE and the code following the if-statement is executed.

Here is how the logical AND operator looks when used in conjunction with the if-statement.

```
if (age>=18 && citizen==true)
```

You may have noticed that there are no quotes around the true value for the citizen part of the expression. In this case true is not a string, but a Boolean value. Boolean values—true or false—can be held in a Javascript variable and do not need to be quoted.

There is also another "join" operator, the double pipe | |, which creates a logical OR comparison. It tests whether the value of at least one of the conditions is true. If it is, then the code block following the if-statement is executed, otherwise the code is not carried out.

Here is how the logical OR operator looks when used in conjunction with the if-statement.

```
if(age>=18 || citizen==true)
```

Let's get back to our voting example and apply the compound conditional above.

To work this out, we need two variables – *age* and *citizenship*. For *age* the condition is age >= 18, while *citizenship* will assume a Boolean value, citizenship==true.

The body of the statement must now be:

```
<body>
<script language="javascript" type="test/
javascript">

var age=18;
var citizen=true;

if(age>=18 && citizen==true)
   {
document.write("You can vote. <br/>");
   }
```

Now both *age* and *citizen* need to be TRUE before the message "You can vote" is displayed.

Case 2: Add another conditional statement in the code above that will display the message "You are the course instructor!" on the second line when the variable *name* contains the string value "Mark".

The conditional statement will simply test if the value of the variable *name* is the string "Mark".

Below is the complete code to accomplish the above tasks:

CODE LISTING: SIMPLE CONDITIONALS

```
<!DOCTYPE HTML PUBLIC "-//W3C//DTD HTML
4.01//EN"
    "http://www.w3.org/TR/html4/strict.dtd"
    >
<html lang="en">
<head>
    <title>Conditional</title>
</head>
<body>
    <script language="javascript"
type="text/javascript">
        var age = 18;
        var citizen = true;
        if(age>=18 && citizen==true)
        {
            document.write("You can
vote<br/>");
        }

        var name="Mark";

        if(name == "Mark")
        {
            document.write("You are the
course instructor!");
        }
```

```
</script>
</body>
</html>
```

This is how the output will look when viewed in the browser:

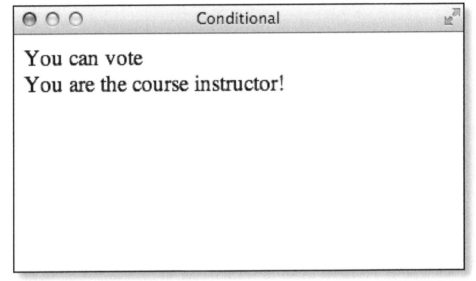

FIGURE 3 - 4

QUESTIONS FOR REVIEW

1. What would be a good definition of a conditional statement?
   a. A statement that conditions your software.
   b. A statement that makes the program branch based on a condition.
   c. A statement that allows the program to make its own decisions.
   d. A statement that conditions the program to allow variables.

2. What does the comparison operator ">=" mean?
   a. Less than or equal to.   c. Equal to.
   b. Greater than or equal to.   d. Equivalent.

3. What does the comparison operator "!=" mean?
   - a. Not equal to.
   - b. Equal to.
   - c. Equivalent.
   - d. Greater than.

4. What comparison operator would you use to create a compound statement which will logically "AND" two statements?
   - a. ++
   - b. --
   - c. ==
   - d. &&

LAB ACTIVITY

1) Create a standard HTML document containing the necessary Javascript <script> tags and attributes.

2) You will implement a program that uses an if-statement. You will evaluate two variables: citizenship, a Boolean; and age, an integer. You will display a message based on evaluation of the variables.

The program must be able to decide whether the user is of voting age and a US citizen and if both conditions are TRUE, will display the first message "You can vote. You are 18 or above and a citizen."

3) If only one condition is TRUE, say age, and then citizenship is FALSE, the message "Sorry, you cannot vote. You are 18 but you are not a citizen." is displayed as second.

4) If both variables for age and citizenships yield FALSE, then the message "Sorry, you cannot vote. You are below 18 and you are not a citizen." is displayed as third.

5) Include another conditional statement that will test if a variable's value is equal to "Mark" and if TRUE, will display the fourth message, "You are the course instructor!"

Following is the expected output:

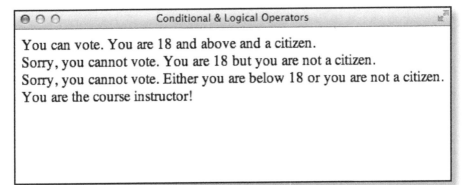

FIGURE 3 - 5

CODE LISTING: LAB ACTIVITY SOLUTION

```
<!DOCTYPE HTML PUBLIC "-//W3C//DTD HTML
4.01//EN"
    "http://www.w3.org/TR/html4/strict.dtd"
    >
<html lang="en">
<head>
    <title>Conditional & Logical
Operators</title>
</head>
<body>
    <script language="javascript"
type="text/javascript">

        var age = 18;
// Variable declaration and initialization
        var citizen = true;
//Boolean variable TRUE

        if(age>=18 && citizen==true)
//Conditional
        {
            document.write("You can vote.
```

```
You are 18 and above and a citizen.<br/>");
        }

        var age = 18;
// Variable declaration and initialization
        var citizen = false;
//Boolean variable FALSE

        if(age>=18 && citizen!=true)
//Conditional
        {
                document.write("Sorry, you
cannot vote. You are 18 but you are not a
citizen.<br/>");
        }

        var age = 18;
// Variable declaration and initialization
        var citizen = false;
//Boolean Variable FALSE

        if(age<=18 && citizen==false)
//Conditional FALSE
        {
                document.write("Sorry, you
cannot vote. Either you are below 18 and
you are not a citizen.<br/>");
        }
var name="Mark";

        if(name == "Mark")
        {
                document.write("You are the
course instructor!");
        }
</script>
</body>
</html>
```

3.2 IF-ELSE-IF STATEMENTS

We are going to continue our look at conditionals in this section as we use conditionals with the **Else** statements.

The if-statement can run through a series of nested conditions that are carried out by setting up the **If-Else-If** which accommodates more complex branching.

Let's create a game score scenario where there is a variable for the highest score and another variable containing the player score.

If the player's score is greater than the high score, the program will display a message that the player beat the high score. However, if the player's score was lower, another message will be displayed indicating that the player did not achieve the high score. In this situation, two variables will have to be declared and initialized. The variable *playerScore* will contain the value 25000 and the variable *highScore* contains the value 10000. What we want to do is set up a conditional that outputs a statement when the *playerScore* variable is greater than the *highScore*.

The if-statement will be:

```
if(playerScore > highScore)
```

Now, if the *playerScore* is greater than the *highScore*, we also want to change *highScore* to the *playerScore* value. So, if the if statement is true, we change the value of *highScore* with:

```
highScore = playerScore;
```

However, if the initial condition is FALSE, we need to use the else statement to output the other message. Using our else statement, the code should be:

```
if(playerScore > highScore)
{
    //Player has high score
    highScore = playerScore;
```

```
document.write("You attained the high
score!");
        } else
        {
document.write("You did not attain the high
score.");
        }
```

Using this conditional, the program will evaluate the condition as TRUE, display the string, and change the *highScore* variable to the *playerScore*. If the *playerScore* variable is lower than 10,000, the if-statement would evaluate as FALSE and the string would output the message within the else statement. The complete code listing is as follows:

```
<!DOCTYPE HTML PUBLIC "-//W3C//DTD HTML
4.01//EN"
    "http://www.w3.org/TR/html4/strict.dtd"
    >
<html lang="en">
<head>
    <title>If-Else-If Condition</title>
</head>
<body>
<script language="javascript" type="text/
javascript">

        var playerScore=25000;
        var highScore=10000;

        if(playerScore > highScore)
            {
                //Player has high score
                highScore = playerScore;

document.write("You attained the high
score!");
            }
        else
```

```
            {
document.write("You did not attain the high
score.");
            }
    </script>
</body>
</html>
```

This is how the output of the above code will look when viewed in the browser:

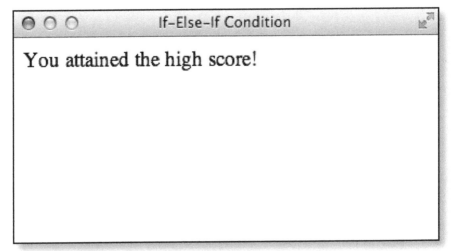

FIGURE 3 - 6

The if-else combination is very useful when you have an either/or situation. However, if you want to create a situation that contains several conditions, you can use a series of if-else-if statements.

In this example, we will practice the use of several conditions. The best practice set for this is a grading scheme.

Case 1: Create a program that will display the equivalent letter grade of students.

You will need two variables: *numericalGrade* and *letterGrade*. *numericalGrade* will be a numerical variable and *letterGrade* will carry a string.

This is how the conditional statement should be written:

```
if(numericalGrade >= 90)
{
letterGrade = "A";
}

else if(numericalGrade >= 80)
    {

    }
```

First, the condition "numericalGrade >= 90" is being evaluated. If it is evaluated as TRUE, the value "A" will be placed in the variable *letterGrade*. However, if the variable is FALSE, the program will move on to the subsequent conditional and evaluate "numericalGrade >=80".

We end the statement with our final conditional block as an else statement. This is because if the *numericalGrade* is lower than a 60, the only option left is the grade "F".

Once the program has run through the if-else-if conditional block, the *letterGrade* value will be displayed to the user.

CODE LISTING: IF-ELSE-IF EXAMPLES

```
<!DOCTYPE HTML PUBLIC "-//W3C//DTD HTML
4.01//EN"
    "http://www.w3.org/TR/html4/strict.dtd"
    >
<html lang="en">
<head>
    <title>Conditionals with Else</title>
</head>
<body>
<script language="javascript" type="text/
javascript">

        var numericalGrade= 95;
```

```
     var letterGrade;

     if(numericalGrade >= 90)
     {
         letterGrade = "A";
     } else if(numericalGrade >= 80)
     {
         letterGrade = "B";
     } else if(numericalGrade >= 70)
     {
         letterGrade = "C";
     } else if(numericalGrade >= 60)
     {
         letterGrade = "D";
     } else
     {
         letterGrade= "F";
     }

     document.write("<br/>Your grade is
" + letterGrade);

   </script>
</body>
</html>
```

This is how the output will appear when viewed in the browser:

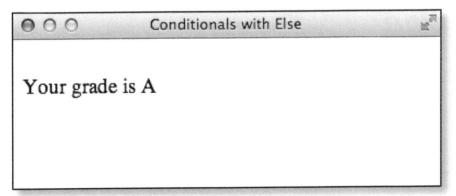

FIGURE 3 - 7

Create a program that will determine and display a student's equivalent letter grade followed by the remark if the student passed, is conditional or failed. Use the following grades obtained and table of equivalent grades and remarks:

Grades obtained: 88, 75, 40, 65, 95.6

Grade	Equivalent Letter Grade	Remarks
90 & up	A	Passed
80-89.99	B	Passed
70-79.99	C	Passed
60-69.99	D	Conditional
59 & below	F	Failed

TABLE 3 - 2

This is how the output should look when viewed in the browser:

When *numericalGrade* is 88:

○ ○ ○   Conditionals with Else

Your grade is B and you Passed.

FIGURE 3 - 8

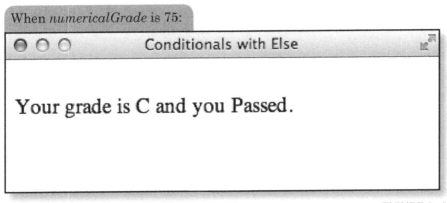

When *numericalGrade* is 75:

Conditionals with Else

Your grade is C and you Passed.

FIGURE 3 - 9

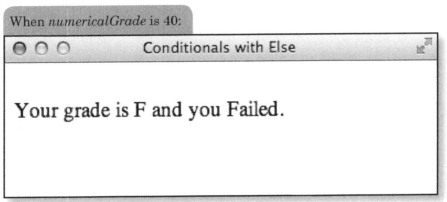

When *numericalGrade* is 40:

Conditionals with Else

Your grade is F and you Failed.

FIGURE 3 - 10

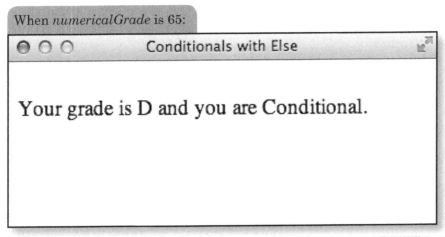

When *numericalGrade* is 65:

Conditionals with Else

Your grade is D and you are Conditional.

FIGURE 3 - 11

When *numericalGrade* is 95.6:

Conditionals with Else

Your grade is A and you Passed.

FIGURE 3 - 12

CODE LISTING: LAB SOLUTION

```
<!DOCTYPE HTML PUBLIC "-//W3C//DTD HTML
4.01//EN"
    "http://www.w3.org/TR/html4/strict.dtd"
    >
<html lang="en">
<head>
    <title>Conditionals with Else</title>
</head>
<body>
<script language="javascript" type="text/
javascript">

        var numericalGrade=88;
        var letterGrade;
        var remark;

        if(numericalGrade >= 90)
            {
                letterGrade = "A";
                remark = "Passed";
            }
```

```
        else if(numericalGrade >= 80)
            {
                letterGrade = "B";
                remark = "Passed";
            }
        else if(numericalGrade >= 70)
            {
                letterGrade = "C";
                remark = "Passed";
            }
        else if (numericalGrade >= 60)
            {
                letterGrade = "D";
                remark = "are Conditional";
            }
        else
            {
                letterGrade= "F";
                remark = "Failed";
            }

        document.write("<br/>Your grade is
" + letterGrade + " " +"and you"+ " " +
remark+".");

    </script>
</body>
</html>
```

1. What does an else statement do?
   a. Execute the next statement if the original conditional statement is true.
   b. Ignore the next statement if the original conditional statement is false.
   c. Execute the next statement if the original conditional statement is false.
   d. Nothing.

2. If you create an if-else-if statement, what happens when the conditional statement is true?
   a. The program continues evaluating the other conditionals.
   b. The program stops running.
   c. The program stops evaluating the other conditionals and moves on.
   d. Nothing.

3. Using variable *studentgrade*, how would you write a statement that tells us a student with a grade higher than 59 passes and those with a grade of 59 or lower fail?
   a. if (studentgrade>59) {document.write ("You passed"); }
   b. if (studentgrade>59) {document.write ("You passed");} else {document.write ("You failed"); }
   c. if (studentgrade>=59) {document.write ("You passed"); } else {document.write ("You failed"); }
   d. if (studentgrade<59) {document.write ("You passed"); } else {document.write ("You failed");}

3.3 SWITCH-CASE-BREAK STATEMENTS

Another way you can test multiple conditions is by using a **switch statement**. A switch statement allows you to test a number of conditions and see if they are true very quickly.

For this section, we will display a string of text based on the case conditions by a variable. We will test the variable *letterGrade*.

The switch-case-break series starts with a switch statement. The switch determines which variable will be evaluated for equality. This is done by writing the code:

```
switch (letterGrade)
```

Once the switch is created, you may list a number of cases that can be tested against the value of the switch variable. If any of the cases are determined to be equivalent to the switch variable, the subsequent case code will be executed and switch-case-break block will be terminated.

Each case should have its own code block that is terminated with a break statement.

If two different cases are supposed to yield the same result, they can be written in series, followed by the code block to be executed. This is a good trapping technique that will ensure all possible cases are accounted for.

It is possible to list multiple case conditions in a series prior to an associated code block and the following code listing will show how it's done. If the value of the switch variable is "a" or "A", the program will execute the corresponding document.write() statement.

```
case "A":
case "a":
document.write("A is an excellent grade!");
break;
```

An almost unlimited number of cases may be written and associated with a single switch. One final element of switch-case-break is the default block. The default block can be used to execute the code if the value of the switch variable is not equal to the value of any of the cases.

Here is the complete code listing:

```
<!DOCTYPE HTML PUBLIC "-//W3C//DTD HTML
4.01//EN"
    "http://www.w3.org/TR/html4/strict.dtd"
    >
<html lang="en">
<head>
    <title>Switch Statements</title>
</head>
<body>
    <script language="javascript"
type="text/javascript">
        var letterGrade = "c";

        switch (letterGrade)
        {
            case "A":
            case "a":
document.write("A is an excellent grade!");
                break;
            case "B":
            case "b":
document.write("B is a good grade!");
                break;
            case "C":
            case "c":
document.write("C is an average grade");
                break;
            case "D":
            case "d":
document.write("D is a low passing grade");
                break;
            case "F":
            case "f":
```

```
document.write("F is a failure.  You must
repeat the course");
                break;
        default:
document.write("Grade not recognized");
        }
    </script>
</body>
</html>
```

This is how the output of the above code listing will look when viewed in the browser:

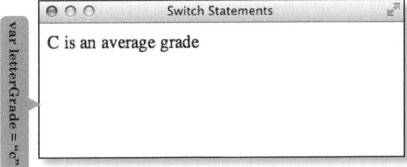

FIGURE 3 - 13

QUESTIONS FOR REVIEW

1. What is a good definition of what a switch statement does?
   a. Tests a number of conditions, one at a time, to see if at least one is true.
   b. Tests one condition case to see if it is true, else it seeks other conditions down the series until it encounters the default case.
   c. Evaluates the switches in your program.
   d. Breaks the program up.

2. What does the default case do?
   a. Runs when everything matches.
   b. Runs when two variables are equal.
   c. Runs when nothing matches.
   d. Runs when an if-else statement is used.

3. What happens if you forget a break statement after a case?
   a. The program stops.
   b. The program ignores the other cases.
   c. The program stops evaluating the other conditionals and moves on.
   d. The program executes the other cases until a break is reached.

CHAPTER 3 LAB EXERCISE

Create a basic HTML document structure. Add Javascript code that will determine and display the following:

1) Declare a variable called *age* and assign it the value 35. Using the chart below, write an **if-else-if** routine that will display the correct output according to the values listed on the table.

Age Range	Output
Under 18	"You're just a pup!"
18-29	"Welcome to young adulthood...have fun now (while you can!)"
30-39	"It's time to get serious about career and family."
40-49	"Time to start thinking about retirement. Make sure you're saving."
50-59	"Enjoy your life now! You've done well."
60 or Over	"60 is the new 40. Do something exciting!"

TABLE 3 - 3

Test your code. Try changing the value in age and make sure it still works correctly.

2) Declare and initialize the following variables:
   discountCode, value =C;
   discountRate, value = 0 ;
   amountOfSale, value = 27.95;

3) Use **switch-case-break** to determine the value of *discountRate* based on the *discountCode* and *amountOfSale*. Use the following table of discount values for reference:

Discount Code	Discount Rate
A	0.325
B	0.050
C	0.075
D	0.100

TABLE 3 - 4

> **Note:** You may get a number with quite a few decimal places to the right of the decimal point. We'll talk about rounding numbers later in the course.

Adjust your code so it still works if the discount code were to be entered as a lower case letter.

CHAPTER 3 LAB EXERCISE SOLUTION

This is how the output will look when viewed in the browser:

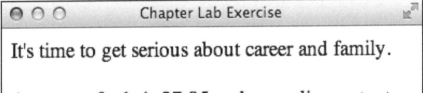

It's time to get serious about career and family.

Amount of sale is 27.95 and your discount rate is 0.075 and your discounted sale amount is 25.853749999999998

FIGURE 3 - 14

```
<!DOCTYPE HTML PUBLIC "-//W3C//DTD HTML
4.01//EN"
    "http://www.w3.org/TR/html4/strict.dtd"
>
<html lang="en">
<head>
    <title>Chapter Lab Exercise</title>
</head>
<body>
<script language="javascript" type="text/
javascript">

        var age=35;

        if(age < 18)
            {
                document.write("You're just
a pup!<br/>");
            }
        else if(age >= 18 && age<= 29)
            {
                document.write("Welcome to
young adulthood... Have fun now (while you
can!)<br/>");
            }
        else if(age >= 30 && age<= 39)
            {
                document.write("It's
time to get serious about career and
family.<br/>");
            }
        else if (age>=50 && age<=59)
            {
                document.write("Enjoy your life
now! You've done well.<br/>");
```

```
        }
        else if (age >= 60)
            {
                document.write("60 is the
new 40. Do something exciting!<br/>");
            }
        else
            {
                document.write("C'mon tell
me you age. <br/>");
            }

var discountCode="C";
    var amountOfSale=27.95;

    switch (discountCode)
        {
            case "A":
            case "a":
                discountRate=0.325;
                document.write("Amount
of sale is "+ amountOfSale + "
and your discount rate is " +
discountRate + " and your discounted
sale amount is " + (amountOfSale-
(amountOfSale*discountRate)));
                break;
            case "B":
            case "b":
                discountRate=0.050;
                document.write("Amount
of sale is "+ amountOfSale + "
and your discount rate is " +
discountRate + " and your discounted
sale amount is " + (amountOfSale-
(amountOfSale*discountRate)));
                break;
            case "C":
```

```
                case "c":
                        discountRate=0.075;
                        document.write("Amount
of sale is "+ amountOfSale + "
and your discount rate is " +
discountRate + " and your discounted
sale amount is " + (amountOfSale-
(amountOfSale*discountRate)));
                        break;
                case "D":
                case "d":
                        discountRate=0.100;
                        document.write("Amount
of sale is "+ amountOfSale + "
and your discount rate is " +
discountRate + " and your discounted
sale amount is " + (amountOfSale-
(amountOfSale*discountRate)));
                        break;

                default:
                        document.write("Discount
Rate not recognized");
                }

    </script>
</body>
</html>
```

CHAPTER 3 SUMMARY

In chapter 3 we discussed conditional statements. We talked about the simple if condition, the if-else-if condition and the switch-case-break statement.

In the next chapter we will be explaining how to create dialog boxes in Javascript. Dialog boxes can alert the user and also allow a user to enter data.

CHAPTER 4

DIALOG BOXES

CHAPTER OBJECTIVES:

- You will be able to create "alert", "prompt" and "confirm" dialog boxes.
- You will be able to use data entered in a dialog box in an application.

4.1 THREE TYPES OF DIALOG BOXES

In this section, we are going to review the three types of dialog boxes that are available to Javascript programmers. These dialog boxes pop up in front of the browser windows and force the user to acknowledge them before they can continue using the web application. Javascript dialogs are sometimes referred to as *modal* dialogs since they require the user to respond before doing anything else within the browser.

The first dialog box that we'll look at is the **alert box,** which is the easiest to implement. An alert box displays a message window that shows the strings placed or value assigned to the variable within the Javascript alert command.

The alert box is set up by using the command **alert**, followed by parentheses:

```
alert("Have a nice day!");
```

Creating the alert box is really very simple. In fact, below is the complete code listing for a "Have a nice day!" alert box:

```
<!DOCTYPE HTML PUBLIC "-//W3C//DTD HTML
4.01//EN"
    "http://www.w3.org/TR/html4/strict.dtd"
    >
<html lang="en">
<head>
    <title>Dialog Box - Alert</title>
```

```
</head>
<body>
<script language="javascript" type="text/
javascript">
        alert("Have a nice day!");
    </script>
</body>
</html>
```

In the Firefox browser the alert dialog will appear as follows:

FIGURE 4 - 1

In Chrome:

In Internet Explorer:

FIGURE 4 - 3

In Opera:

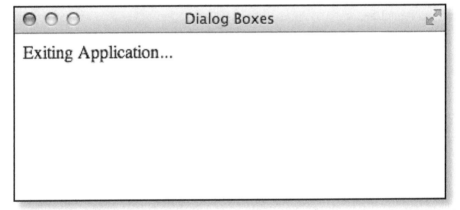

FIGURE 4 - 1

Aside from the straightforward use of the alert command, an "alert" box can also display string values or text through the use of a variable. Rather than writing the string or text inside the parentheses after the *alert* function, you instead designate the string as the value of a variable and call the variable from the *alert* command.

The alert box in this code example displays a string stored in a variable:

```html
<!DOCTYPE HTML PUBLIC "-//W3C//DTD HTML
4.01//EN"
    "http://www.w3.org/TR/html4/strict.dtd"
    >
<html lang="en">
<head>
    <title>Dialog Box - Alert</title>
</head>
<body>
<script language="javascript" type="text/
javascript">
        var message= "Have a nice day! ";
 alert(message);
    </script>
</body>
</html>
```

The previous code listing will show exactly the same output as the previous example.

The second type of dialog box we'll examine is the **confirm box**. A confirm box asks the user a question and then the user supplies the answer by clicking the okay or cancel button displayed in the dialog box itself.

This box is a little more complicated to code than the *alert* box because the users response must be stored in a variable. Commonly this is done via variable assignment. The variable stores a Boolean TRUE or FALSE based on the user's response to the prompt.

To demonstrate, let's use a variable called *confirmation;* initialize its value using the syntax **confirm(" ")**. Inside the double quotes, put the text you want displayed to the user as the confirmation question. The code looks like this:

```
var confirmation = confirm("Do you want to
exit?");
```

If the user clicks "OK", the value "TRUE" will be stored to the variable *confirmation*; conversely, if the user clicks "Cancel", the value "FALSE" will be stored to the variable *confirmation*.

> **The confirm dialog box has two default responses: OK or Cancel**

Let's use a conditional to evaluate the user's response to the prompt and display a message.

We're going to create a routine that will display the string "Exiting Application..." when the user selects "OK"; and will display the string "Staying on the Application..." if the user selects "Cancel".

This is the complete code listing:

```
<!DOCTYPE HTML PUBLIC "-//W3C//DTD HTML
4.01//EN"
    "http://www.w3.org/TR/html4/strict.dtd"
    >
<html lang="en">
<head>
    <title>Dialog Boxes</title>
</head>
<body>
    <script language="javascript"
type="text/javascript">

        var confirmation = confirm("Are you
sure you want to exit?");

        if(confirmation)
            {
                document.write("Exiting
Application...");
            }
        else
            {
                document.write("Staying on
the Application...");
            }
```

```
        </script>
    </body>
</html>
```

This is a screenshot of the confirm dialog box in Chrome:

FIGURE 4 - 5

This is the result when "OK" is clicked:

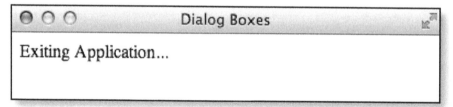

FIGURE 4 - 6

This is the result when "Cancel" is clicked:

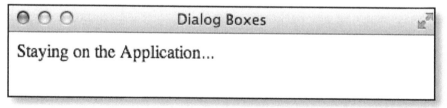

FIGURE 4 - 7

The third type of dialog box is called a **prompt dialog box**. The prompt dialog box allows the user to input data.

Similar to a confirm dialog box, the prompt dialog box will also require the use of a variable to store the user's response.

For our example, we can use the prompt dialog box to ask the user's age. The user then types their response inside the dialog box. The variable *age* will hold the value of whatever the user will input.

The command to implement the prompt dialog box would be:

```
var age = prompt("What is your age", "");
```

Notice that there are two sets of quotation marks inside the parentheses. (These are sometimes refered to as **arguments**.) The second set of quotations allows the developer to supply a default value for the dialog box if they desire.

After the user responds to the prompt dialog, the program should display the string "You are _ years old", the blank being replaced by the value the user enters. Secondly, we'd like it to display on the next line "You can vote" if the age entered is 18 and above.

The complete code listing looks like this:

CODE LISTING: DIALOG BOXES

```
<!DOCTYPE HTML PUBLIC "-//W3C//DTD HTML
4.01//EN"
    "http://www.w3.org/TR/html4/strict.dtd"
    >
<html lang="en">
<head>
    <title>Dialog Boxes</title>
</head>
<body>
    <script language="javascript"
type="text/javascript">

    var age = prompt("What is your age",
"");
document.write("You are " + age + " years
old");
```

```
            if(age >18)
            {
document.write("<br/>You can vote!");
            }
     </script>
</body>
</html>
```

This is how the output of the above code will appear:

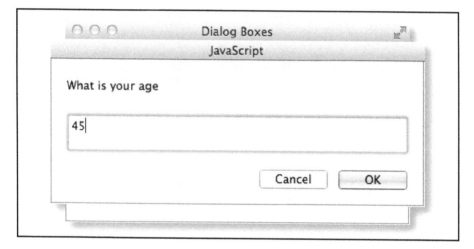

FIGURE 4 - 8

After keying in the value, this is what gets displayed:

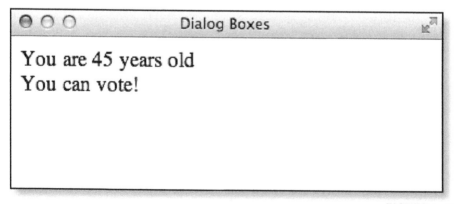

FIGURE 4 - 9

QUESTIONS FOR REVIEW

1. What does the *alert* box do?
   a. Sends a message in the browser that requires no response from the user.
   b. Sends a message in the browser that requires a response from the user.
   c. Sends a message in the webpage that requires a response from the user.
   d. Sends a message in the webpage that requires no response from the user.

2. Which dialog box gives users the ability to respond by clicking the "okay" or "cancel" buttons?
   a. Alert   c. True
   b. Confirm   d. Prompt

3. What box allows the user to enter a string of data?
   a. Alert   c. True
   b. Confirm   d. Prompt

CHAPTER 4 LAB EXERCISE

Create a basic HTML document structure. In the document body, add script tags with the appropriate attributes to add Javascript code.

1) Using the correct dialog box code, create a box that contains the text "What is your dog's age in human years?" The user should be able to type their response directly into the dialog box.

Store the user's response in a variable called *dogAgeInHumanYears*.

Multiply the *dogAgeInHumanYears* value by seven and store in a variable called *dogAgeInDogYears*.

2) Use an *alert()* dialog box to output the result with the text "Your dog is X years old in dog years."

3) After the user acknowledges the *alert()* box, another dialog should appear and ask the user "Shall I exit the program?" This dialog should display two buttons allowing the user to either confirm or cancel.

If the user confirms, the text "Exiting Dog Years Calculator" should appear. If the user cancels, the text "Cancelling Exit" shall appear.

CODE LISTING: CHAPTER LAB EXERCISE SOLUTION

```
<!DOCTYPE HTML PUBLIC "-//W3C//DTD HTML
4.01//EN"
    "http://www.w3.org/TR/html4/strict.dtd"
    >
<html lang="en">
<head>
    <title>Dialog Boxes-Chapter Lab
Exercise</title>
</head>
<body>
    <script language="javascript"
type="text/javascript">

        var dogAgeInHumanYears =
prompt("What is your dog's age in human
years?");
        var dogAgeInDogYears = 0;
        dogAgeInDogYears=dogAgeInHumanYears
* 7;

            alert("Your dog is " +
dogAgeInDogYears + " years old in dog
years.");

        var confirmation = confirm("Shall I
exit the program?")
        if(confirmation)
            {
                document.write("Exiting Dog
Years Calculator");
            }
        else
            {
```

```
            document.write("Cancelling
Exit.");
            }
    </script>
</body>
</html>
```

This is how the outputs of the above code will look:

First dialog box, viewed in Opera:

FIGURE 4 - 10

First dialog box, viewed in Firefox:

FIGURE 4 - 11

Second dialog box, viewed in Firefox:

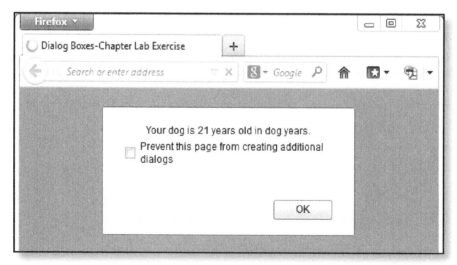

FIGURE 4 - 12

Third dialog box, viewed in Opera:

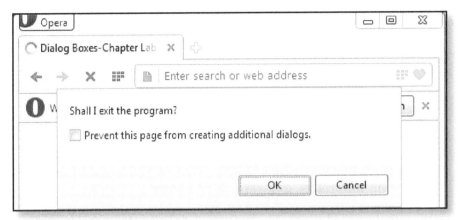

FIGURE 4 - 13

This is the browser's display after the user has clicked "OK", viewed in Chrome:

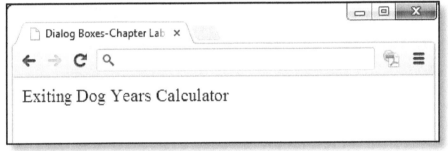

FIGURE 4 - 14

This is the browser's display after the user has clicked "Cancel", viewed in Chrome:

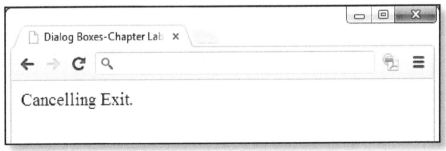

FIGURE 4 - 15

CHAPTER 4 SUMMARY

In this chapter, we discussed how to use Javascript to create dialog boxes that pop up in a browser window. You learned how to implement the *prompt*, *confirm* and *alert* boxes.

We also discussed how to use the user-supplied data in the *prompt* and *confirm* boxes to output strings on the website. You learned how to use conditional statements to display string outputs in the browser after clicking a response in the confirm box.

In chapter 5 we will be discussing how to create loops using Javascript. Loops are one of the most important aspects of programming in any language.

CHAPTER 5
NOW WE'RE ITERATING!
LOOPS IN JAVASCRIPT

CHAPTER OBJECTIVES:
- You will be able to implement while and do-while loops.
- You will be able to create for-loops.
- You will be able to apply loops in practical situations or cases.

5.1 WHILE-LOOPS AND DO-WHILE LOOPS

In this section we will be discussing loops. Loops are important facets of any programming language. With loops you can repeat a certain code block, allowing that code to repeatedly execute until a satisfactory condition is met. Every time the code is executed, it is referred to as an iteration through the loop.

Loops are great for a number of tasks when programming, including receiving user-input data or causing a program to read, parse, and output a lengthy document.

In this section we are going to review **while**-loops and **do-while** loops. To demonstrate loops, let's create a loop that will output the series of numbers from one to 100.

We'll start with the while-loop.

A while-loop is similar to a conditional statement in the sense that it evaluates a condition in the program and if the condition is "TRUE", the code block associated with the loop will run.

We must start by identifying a loop counter variable. Let's use x. With each iteration of the loop, the counter will be compared within a continuation condition. If that condition evaluates as TRUE, the loop will continue to iterate. If it evaluates as FALSE the loop will cease running. If you set up a loop where the continuation condition is always true, you would be creating an infinite loop that will eventually crash your program. For this example, the variable declared is x and its value set to so that the loop iterates 100 times. The syntax for the while-loop is:

```
var x=1;
while (continuation condition)
{
    ...code to execute
}
```

A specific example is:

```
while (x < 101)
```

Following this line is a code block which describes what to do if the condition in the while-statement is "TRUE". Let us instruct the program to write or display the value of the variable x. The command set would look like this:

```
{
        document.write (x + "<br/>");
```

We concatenated a line break tag to the output to keep it readable and neat.

Increasing the value of the variable x by one will change the value of the variable with each iteration of the loop. To increment x, the code should read:

```
        x++;
}
```

After each iteration of the loop, the Javascript interpreter will test the value of x in the continuation condition. In this case, the loop will continue to iterate if $x < 101$ evaluates as true. Once the value of x reaches 101, the continuation condition will evaluate as FALSE and the loop will cease.

This is how the complete loop is coded:

CODE LISTING: WHILE-LOOP

```
var x=1;
while(x < 101)
        {
                document.write(x + "<br/>");
                x++;
        }
```

The value for x is being compared to 101 because if it is compared to 100, the loop will only iterate up to 99 and not 100.

The complete code set to run the routine follows:

Code Listing: Display 1 to 100

```
<!DOCTYPE html>

<html>
<head>
    <title>While-Loop</title>
</head>

<body>
    <script language="Javascript"
type="text/javascript">
        var x = 1;
        while(x < 101)
        {
                document.write(x + "<br/>");
                x++;
        }
    </script>
</body>
</html>
```

> In this example, the loop is going to count to 100, so we want to make sure it only iterates through the loop 100 times.

```
● ○ ○                While-Loop                    ⤢

1
2
3
4
5
6
7
8
9
```

FIGURE 5 - 1

Scroll down and this is what you will
see at the bottom of the browser:

```
95
96
97
98
99
100
```

FIGURE 5 - 2

Do-while loops function in a similar manner as while-loops, only they follow a different syntax. The one functional difference of a do-while loop is that it is guaranteed to iterate at least once—even if the continuation condition is initially false.

You start a do-while loop with the do-statement and end the loop with the while-statement. This means that the condition is tested at the end of the loop, and if it is evaluated as TRUE, the loop will continue to iterate. This is an example of a do-while loop.

CODE LISTING: DO-WHILE LOOP

```
window.onload = function()
{
var y=0;
        do
        {
            document.write(y + "<br/>");
            y++;
        } while(y < 101);
}
```

Here is the result of the do-while loop executing in Firefox:

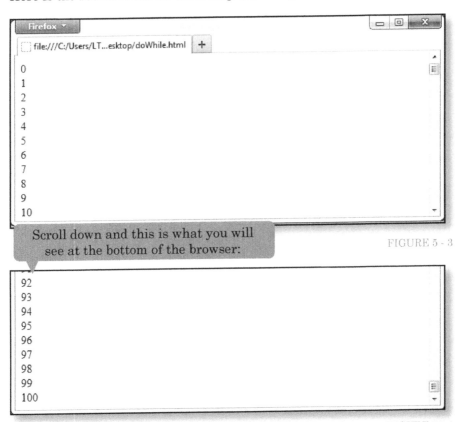

FIGURE 5 - 3

Scroll down and this is what you will see at the bottom of the browser:

FIGURE 5 - 4

In this example, the loop will iterate once, then the condition will be evaluated. When the while-loop's continuation condition yields FALSE, the loop's associated code block will not be executed and there will be no further iterations.

CODE LISTING: WHILE AND DO-WHILE LOOPS

```
<!DOCTYPE HTML PUBLIC "-//W3C//DTD HTML
4.01//EN"
    "http://www.w3.org/TR/html4/strict.dtd"
    >
<html lang="en">
<head>
    <title>While Loops</title>
</head>
<body>
    <script language="javascript"
type="text/javascript">
        var x = 1;
        //Loop that counts to 100
        while(x < 101)
        {
            document.write(x + "<br/>");
            x++;
        }
        document.write("##############
##########<br/>");
//Do-while...

        var y=150;
        do
        {
            document.write(y + "<br/>");
            y++;
        } while(y < 101);
    </script>
</body>
</html>
```

The following screenshot is the output of the previous code. Notice how the do-while loop executes once and stops because the condition is false.

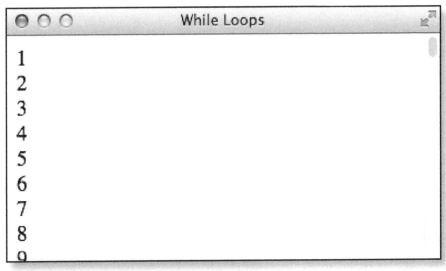

FIGURE 5 - 5

Scroll down and this is what you will see at the bottom of the browser:

FIGURE 5 - 6

1. How does the while-loop function?
   a. Loops while a certain condition is "TRUE".
   b. Loops while a certain condition is "FALSE".
   c. Loops when the program is over.
   d. Loops while another program is running.

2. What loop do you use if you want to guarantee the loop will iterate at least once before it tests the condition?
   a. While-loop.
   b. Do-while loop.
   c. For-loop.
   d. If-then loop.

3. How does a do-while loop differ from a while-loop?
   a. The condition is set at the beginning.
   b. The condition is set at the end.
   c. There is no condition.
   d. There is no difference.

5.2 FOR-LOOPS AND PRACTICAL APPLICATION OF A LOOP

For-loops are compact loops that allow you to set the variable, the condition, and the continuation condition (or counter) within the loop command itself. They save time, are easy to decipher and create less code in the long run.

This is what a for-loop looks like:

```
for(var i=100; i > -1; i=i-5)
```

There are three elements to a for-loop command.

First is the declaration of the counter variable and the assignment of its initial value.

In the above example, it is *var i=100;*

The second part of the for-loop is the continuation condition which will determine how many times the loop will iterate; here, the loop will iterate as long as the variable is greater than -1, that is *i >-1* in the above example.

The third and last element of a for-loop is the "counter". The counter determines how the counter variable will change with each iteration of the loop. In the above example, the loop will start from 100 and count down by fives, *i=i-5,* for each iteration. Based on this, the loop will iterate—or loop—21 times.

Care must be observed when using for-loops, as it is very easy to create an infinite loop if you set the counter incorrectly.

Here is the complete code for the previous for-loop example:

CODE LISTING: FOR LOOPS

```
<!DOCTYPE HTML PUBLIC "-//W3C//DTD HTML
4.01//EN"
    "http://www.w3.org/TR/html4/strict.dtd"
    >
<html lang="en">
<head>
    <title>For Loops</title>
</head>
<body>
    <script language="javascript"
type="text/javascript">
        for(var i=100; i > -1; i=i-5)
        {
            document.write(i + "<br/>");
        }

        /* Endless Loop
        for(var i = 0; i >= 0; i++)
        {
            document.write(i + "<br/>");
        }
        */
    </script>
</body>
</html>
```

A break has been included in the output command so that each number is displayed on the next line. Notice in the comment portion where an example of an endless loop code is shown.

This is how the output will appear in a browser:

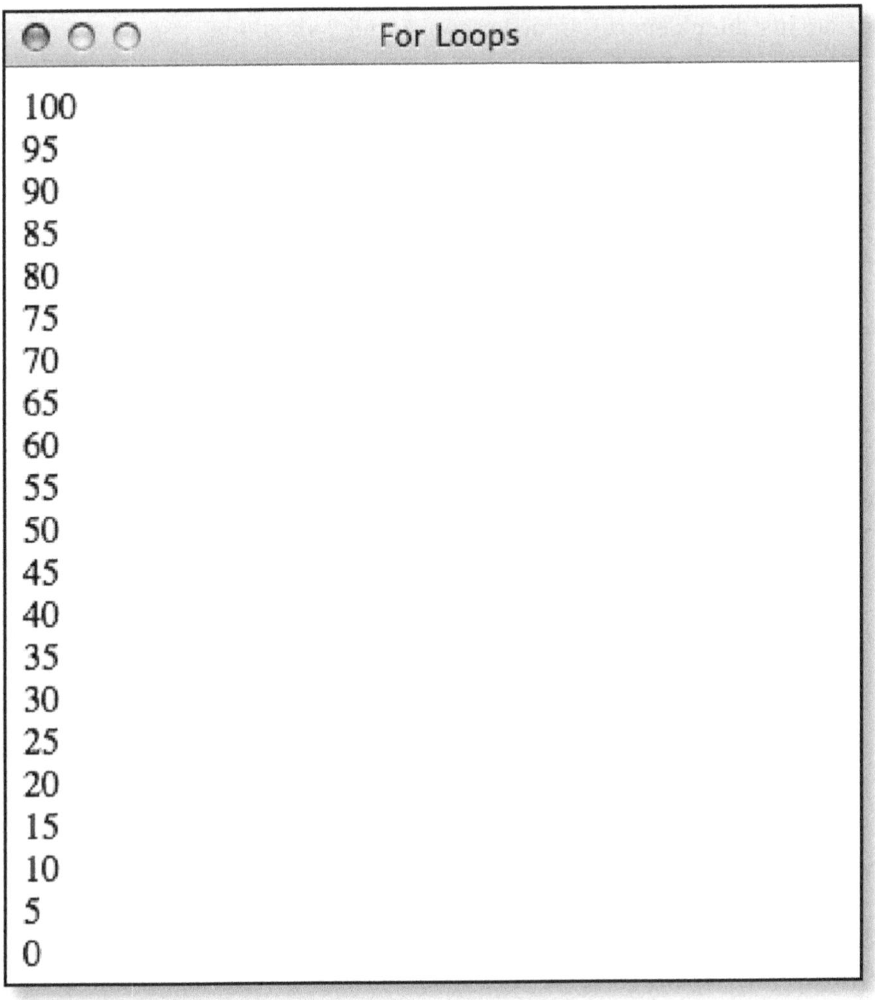

```
┌──────────────────────────────────────────────┐
│  ⊖ ○ ○              For Loops                 │
├──────────────────────────────────────────────┤
│  100                                           │
│  95                                            │
│  90                                            │
│  85                                            │
│  80                                            │
│  75                                            │
│  70                                            │
│  65                                            │
│  60                                            │
│  55                                            │
│  50                                            │
│  45                                            │
│  40                                            │
│  35                                            │
│  30                                            │
│  25                                            │
│  20                                            │
│  15                                            │
│  10                                            │
│  5                                             │
│  0                                             │
└──────────────────────────────────────────────┘
```

FIGURE 5 - 7

Loops are one of the most useful constructs in programming. They can be used in a variety of practical applications.

In this section, we are going to combine looping with the prompt dialog concept. The prompt dialog concept was introduced in the previous chapter to create a program that allows the user to input their favorite bands. This application of loops will help demonstrate one practical use of loops.

Let's use a narrative algorithm to show how events will take place in our program.

Declare a variable which will receive the user's input. Call it *ui*. Assign it a null value (meaning, do not put any string or numeric value inside, just blank space). Code for step 1 and 2 should be:

```
var ui = "";
```

Introduce the loop. The loop will continue to run if the value of *ui* is not "xxx". The code is:

```
while(ui != "xxx")
```

Write the code that will be executed when the continuation condition is evaluated as TRUE and place the code inside the while-loop. Nest a conditional within the loop that will test the user input and react accordingly. The combined code for step 4 and 5 should be:

```
{
ui= prompt("Enter a name of one of your
favorite bands. Enter xxx to stop");
if(ui != "xxx")
        {
document.write(ui + "<br/>");
        }
}
```

End the program code.

The complete code listing for the above algorithm is:

CODE LISTING: LOOPING INPUT

```
<!DOCTYPE HTML PUBLIC "-//W3C//DTD HTML
4.01//EN"
    "http://www.w3.org/TR/html4/strict.dtd"
    >
<html lang="en">
<head>
    <title>Looping Input</title>
```

```
</head>
<body>
    <script language="javascript"
type="text/javascript">
        var ui = "";
        while(ui != "xxx")
        {
            ui= prompt("Enter a name of
one of your favorite bands. Enter xxx to
stop");
            if(ui != "xxx")
            {
                document.write(ui +
"<br/>");
            }
        }
    </script>
</body>
</html>
```

To recap, the browser will prompt the user to enter a band name. If the user enters a band name, the if-statement routine will cause the band name to be displayed in the browser. The loop will continue to ask until the user enters "xxx". Only then will the loop stop.

Remember that when the prompt boxes appear, clicking "Cancel" will simply display "null" in the browser and will not end the program routine. Typing in "xxx" will end the program.

Following are the outputs of the program showing the stages as each band is typed in until "xxx":

FIGURE 5 - 8

Example Input 1:

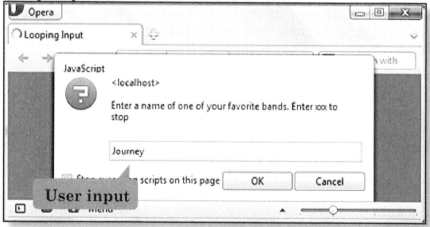

FIGURE 5 - 9

Example Input 2:

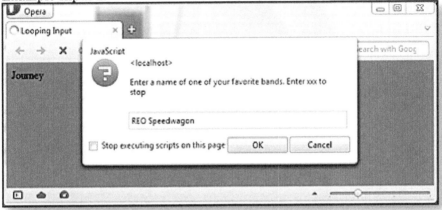

FIGURE 5 - 10

Example Input 3:

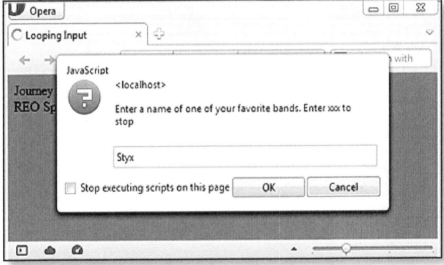

FIGURE 5 - 11

Example Input 4:

FIGURE 5 - 12

Example Input 5:

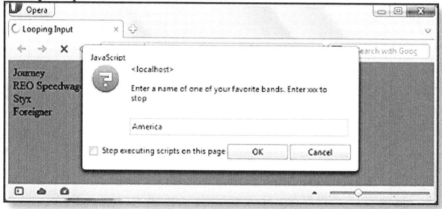

FIGURE 5 -13

Example Input 6:

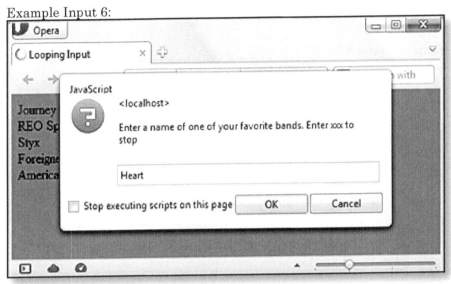

FIGURE 5 - 14

Example Input 7:

FIGURE 5 - 15

Example Input 8:

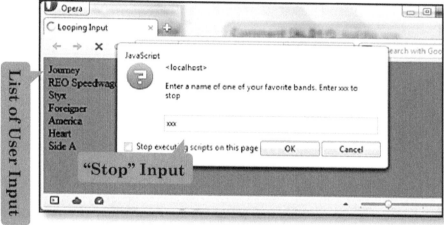

FIGURE 5 - 16

Example final:

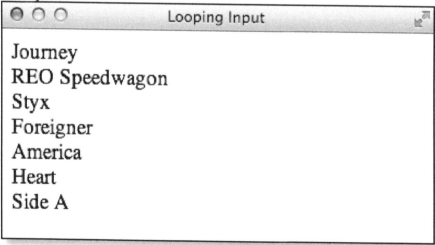

FIGURE 5 - 17

QUESTIONS FOR REVIEW

1. What is the first part of a for-loop?
   a. The condition.
   b. The counter.
   c. The loop.
   d. The initialization.

CHAPTER 5 LAB EXERCISE

LAB EXERCISE 1:

1. Create a basic HTML5 document structure. In the document body, add script tags with the appropriate attributes to add Javascript code.

2. Create a while-loop that counts backwards by fives, from 500 to zero. Output the results with a break between each line.

3. Create a second loop that is a do-while loop. Design the loop so that the initial condition is "FALSE". Observe that the loop will still iterate one time even if the next condition is initially false. Answers will vary.

4. Create a for-loop that outputs the words "I can count... wow!" 10 times. Each time the content is displayed it should be preceded by the number of the iteration. The first iteration should output "1. I can count...wow!", the second "2. I can count...wow!" and so on.

LAB EXERCISE 2:

Hints:
1) *parseFloat()* - parses decimal number inputted
2) *parseInt()* - parses integer number inputted
3) *Math.round()* - to round-off numeric values

In a new HTML5 document, create a program that prompts the user for an interest rate (entered as a decimal such as .05 for 5%); an amount of money invested and a term (in months). Using these values, create a list in the document window that displays how much money the user has earned each month in interest and what their new total is.

The interest accrued each month:
*totalMoney * interestRate*

See the browser output below for an approximation of how the result should look.

The total each month:
*totalMoney + (interestRate * totalMoney)*

LAB EXERCISE 1 SOLUTION

This is how the output should appear:

FIGURE 5 - 18

112 *Javascript for Beginners*

Scroll down and this is what you will
see at the bottom of the browser:

```
50
45
40
35
30
25
20
15
10
5
0
```

FIGURE 5 - 19

This is the output of the other two exercises

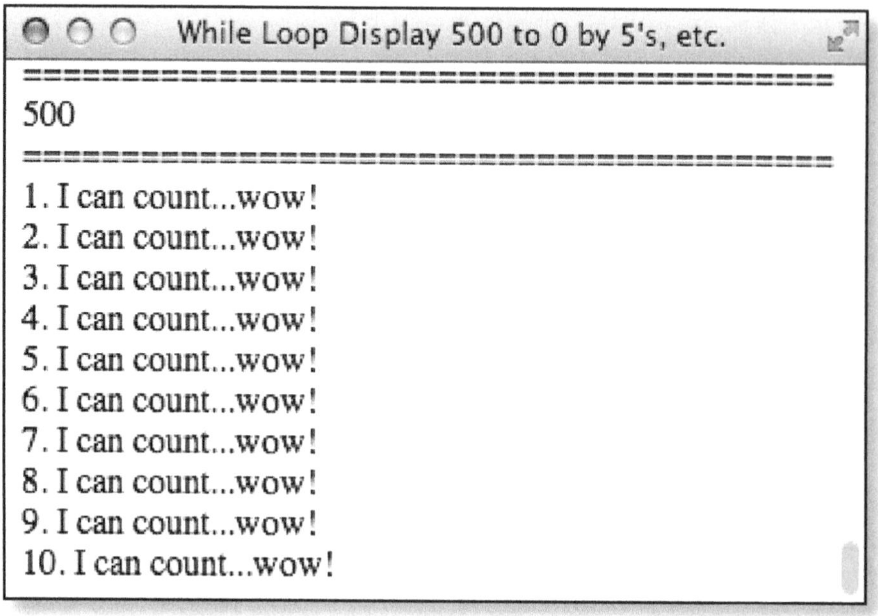

```
○ ○ ○     While Loop Display 500 to 0 by 5's, etc.     ⊠
===========================================
500
===========================================
1. I can count...wow!
2. I can count...wow!
3. I can count...wow!
4. I can count...wow!
5. I can count...wow!
6. I can count...wow!
7. I can count...wow!
8. I can count...wow!
9. I can count...wow!
10. I can count...wow!
```

FIGURE 5 - 20

CODE LISTING: LAB EXERCISE 1

```html
<!DOCTYPE html>
<html>
<head>
    <title>While Loop Display 500 to 0 by
5's, etc. </title>
</head>

<body>
<script language="javascript" type="text/
javascript">
        var x=500;

        while(x > -1)
        {
            document.write(x + "<br/>");
            x=x-5;
```

```
        }
        document.write
("==========================================
");

        var y=500;
        do
        {
            document.write("<br/>" + y +
"<br/>");
            y++;
        } while(y < 500);

        document.write
("==========================================
= <br/>");

        for(var i=1; i < 11; i++)
        {
            document.write(i + "." + " "
+"I can count...wow! <br/>");
        }
</script>
</body>
</html>
```

LAB EXERCISE 2 SOLUTION

This is how each output will look:

Input interest in decimal, viewed in Firefox:

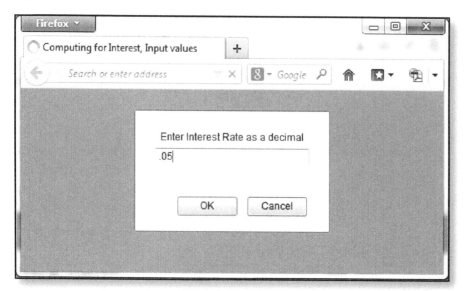

FIGURE 5 - 21

Input number of months, viewed in Chrome:

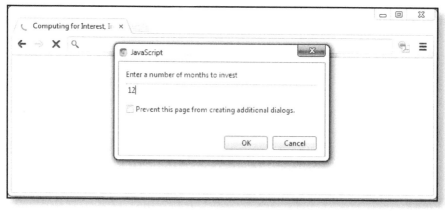

FIGURE 5 - 22

Input amount invested, viewed in Opera:

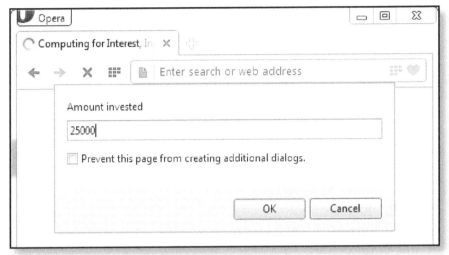

FIGURE 5 - 23

Display interest and total money earned for each of the months:

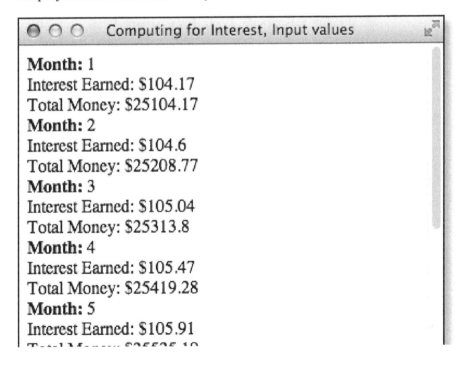

FIGURE 5 - 24

Scroll down and this is what you will
see at the bottom of the browser:

Month: 9
Interest Earned: $107.69
Total Money: $25953.28
Month: 10
Interest Earned: $108.14
Total Money: $26061.42
Month: 11
Interest Earned: $108.59
Total Money: $26170.01
Month: 12
Interest Earned: $109.04
Total Money: $26279.05

FIGURE 5 - 25

CODE LISTING: LAB EXERCISE 2

```
<!DOCTYPE html>

<html lang="en">
<head>
    <title>Computing for Interest, Input
values</title>
<html lang="en">
<head>
    <title>Display Simple Interest</title>
</head>
<body>
    <script language="javascript"
type="text/javascript">
        var interestRate = prompt("Enter
Interest Rate as a decimal" , "");
        var term = prompt("Enter a number
of months to invest", "");
```

```javascript
        var amountInvested = prompt("Amount
invested", "");

        //Convert the strings to values
        interestRate =
parseFloat(interestRate);
        term = parseInt(term);
        amountInvested =
parseInt(amountInvested);

        //Convert Interest Rate to Monthly
accrual
        interestRate = interestRate/12;

        //HINT:  Use Math.round() to round
off values
        // (Math.round()*100)/100 will give
you two decimal places

        for(month = 1; month < term+1 ;
month++)
        {
            document.
write("<strong>Month:</strong> " + month+
"<br>");
            document.write("Interest
Earned: $" + Math.round
((interestRate*amountInvested)*100)/100);
            document.write("<br/>");
            amountInvested = amountInvested
+ (interestRate*amountInvested);
            document.write("Total Money: $"
+ Math.round(amountInvested*100)/100);
            document.write("<br/>");
        }
    </script>
</body>
</html>
```

CHAPTER 5 SUMMARY

In this chapter we discussed loops. A loop is an important element of programming that permits lines of code to execute in a program as many times as the condition allows. You learned how to use while-loops, do-while loops and for-loops.

We also reviewed how to use loops in a practical way. In this instance, a loop was used to allow the user to input data that would appear in the page. The loop would continue iterating as long as the user did not type in the string "xxx".

In chapter 6, we will discuss functions. Functions are indispensable elements of programming that will allow you to create blocks of reusable code you can call at your convenience.

CHAPTER 6

CODING JAVASCRIPT FUNCTIONS

CHAPTER OBJECTIVES:

- You will be able to write and call a function.
- You will be able to create a separate file for functions and link to it.
- You will be able to pass a value to a function.
- You will be able to have a function return a value.
- You will be able to use an event to trigger a function.

6.1 FUNCTION INTRODUCTION

In this chapter, we are going to discuss how to create and use functions. Functions are small blocks of code that can be called and reused within the program and by external routines as well.

There are two components of a function. There is the **function declaration**, which defines the function and its code. Then there is the **function call**. The function call is the instance the function is directed to run or be executed.

To use a function, first it must be defined and given a name. An example of a function name is *displayName*.

The syntax for defining a function is:

```
function displayName()
```

The actual code associated with the function is written in a code block surrounded by curly brackets.

```
{
document.write ("John Doe");
}
```

Functions may be created within the same file in which they are called.

Functions are commonly written within <script> tags in the head of the HTML document and are accessible throughout the program.

For example, let's write out a routine that will display a first and last name. In this case, the function is defined and called within the same document.

CODE LISTING: FUNCTION CALLED FROM WITHIN THE SAME PAGE

```html
<!DOCTYPE html>

<html>
<head>
    <title>Page Title</title>
    <script language="javascript">
    function displayName()
        {
              document.write("John Doe");
        }
    </script>
</head>
<body onload="displayName()">
</body>
</html>
```

onload is an event which implements the function *displayName()* once the page is loaded. We'll cover events in more detail later in the chapter.

This is how the output of the previous code will appear in a browser:

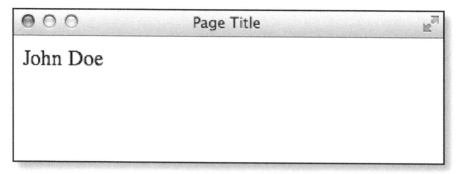

FIGURE 6 - 1

122   *Javascript for Beginners*

However, the most efficient way of using functions is to create a separate
file that contains the function code. This method allows you to use
the functions you create in multiple programs rather than in just one
program. It also makes your code easier to maintain as you can improve
the implementation of a function without editing your HTML.

To define functions in a separate file, create a blank text file and save
it with the .js file extension. Inside that file, define your functions using
the structure that was previously demonstrated. In this example, two
functions are created.

First function routine is displaying a string outright:

```
function displayName()
{
    document.write("Hello there ^-^");
}
```

The second routine will use a variable to display a string appended with a
numeric variable's value:

```
function displayscore()
{
    displayScore = 1000;
document.write("<br/>Player score: " +
playerScore);
}
```

Once you have written your functions, save the file as *functions.js*.

The complete code for the *functions.js* file is:

```
function displayGreeting()
{
    document.write("Hello there! ^-^
<br/>");
}

function displayScore()
```

```
{
playerScore = 1000;
document.write("<br/>Player score is: " +
playerScore);
}
```

You will note that script tags are not necessary for the external file.

To call a function from a separate file, you need to include the file using a script tag. Your script tag must include the source attribute with a value set to the name of the file that includes your Javascript functions. A complete example of the script tag:

```
<script language="javascript" type="text/
javascript" src="functions.js"></script>
```

In this case, the external functions are held in a file called functions.js. This file name is in fact arbitrary—the file could be named anything as long as the extension is .js.

Functions are called by simply writing out the function name and following it with a set of parentheses. In this example, the functions are called and a break is used to separate the two outputs. Putting the codes above together, the complete code listing is:

CODE LISTING: CALLING FUNCTIONS FROM A SEPARATE FILE

```
<!DOCTYPE html>

<head>
    <title>Functions</title>
    <script language="javascript"
type="text/javascript" src="functions.
js"></script>
</head>
<body>
<script language="javascript" type="text/
```

```
javascript">
        displayGreeting();
        displayScore();
    </script>
</body>
</html>
```

Make sure that the file functions.js and the HTML containing the code are in the same folder; otherwise you have to make a relative reference where the separate Javascript file is located (example: /code/functions.js)

This is the output of the code with functions that were called from a separate document.

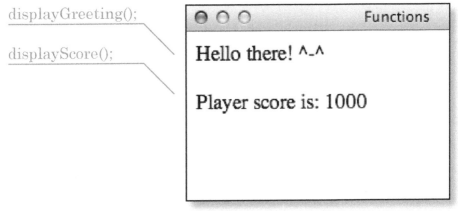

FIGURE 6 - 2

In the next section, we will discuss how to send values between the caller and the function.

1. What are the two parts of a function?
   a. A function call and a function loop.
   b. A function definition and a function loop.
   c. A function call and a function definition.
   d. A function definition and object.

2. How do you declare a function?
   a. Write the keyword function and name of function.
   b. Name of function.
   c. Just function.
   d. Name of Javascript file.

 LAB ACTIVITY

LAB ACTIVITY: CALLING THE FUNCTION—DISPLAYNAME ()

1) Display Name:

In this activity, we will create a function that will be called within the HTML5 document with the aid of an onload event.

1.1) Create a basic HTML5 document.

In the document heading, insert a function called *displayMyName()*. Populate the function with two *document.write()* commands; the first one must contain your name as the string value to be displayed:

```
<head>
    <title>Page Title</title>
    <script language="javascript">

    function displayMyName()
        {
```

```
        document.write("replace this
string with your name... <br/> <br/>"); //
You will have to replace the string values
in this line with your name

While the second document.write line will
display the string value "is A - W- E - S -
O - M - E -!".

        document.write("is   A-W-E-S-O-
M-E-!");
        }
```

1.2) Include an onload event in the body of the document which will call the function.

```
<body onload="displayMyName()">
</body>
```

1.3) Close the script tag and run the code. Your output should be similar to this:

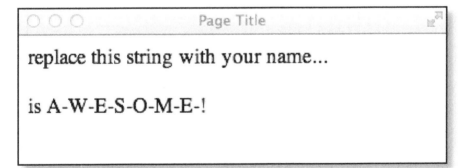

FIGURE 6 - 3

Remember to tweak the function displayName() in your code. Replace the existing string value with your name such that it will be what will get displayed in the output when ran.

Display Name:

```
<!DOCTYPE html>

<html>
<head>
    <title>Page Title</title>
    <script language="javascript">

    function displayMyName()
        {
            document.write("replace this
string with your name... <br/> <br/>"); //
You will have to replace the string values
in this line with your name

            document.write("is  A-W-E-S-O-
M-E-!");
        }
    </script>
</head>

<body onload="displayMyName()">
</body>
</html>
```

LAB ACTIVITY: CALLING FUNCTION—DISPLAYSPORTS ()

2) Display Sports:

In this activity, we will call a function created outside of the HTML5 document but called from within the HTML5 document body.

2.1) Create another basic HTML5 document. In the heading, just underneath the title tags, include Javascript elements to instruct where the .js file source named *attachment.js* is.

```
<script language="javascript" type="text/
javascript" src="attachment.js"></script>
```

The source file, called attachment.js, will be called within the body of the HTML5 document. The call function code would be:

```
<body>
    <script language="javascript"
type="text/javascript">
        displaySport();
        displayStatistic();
    </script>
</body>
```

2.2) Complete the HTML5 document and save.

2.3) Create another document with the filename *attachment.js*. It must contain the two functions named *displaySport()* and *displayStatistics()* containing the following codes:

```
function displaySport()
{
    document.write("Basketball and
Baseball... <br/> <br/>");
    document.write("Two A-W-E-S-O-M-E and
very P-O-P-U-L-A-R sports. <br/>");
}

function displayStatistic()
{
    statistic1 = 55;
    statistic2 = 56;
    document.write("<br/>Statistics show
```

```
  " +statistic1+"% and "+statistic2+"%
respective audience patronage!");
  }
```

2.4) Once completed, save the file and run the HTML5 document. Your output should look like:

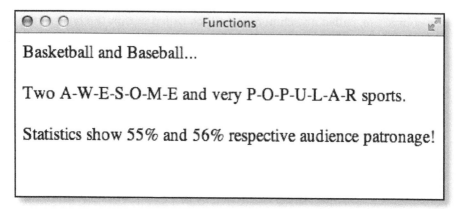

FIGURE 6 - 1

LAB ACTIVITY DISPLAYSPORTS () SOLUTION

2) Display Sports

HTML 5 document:

```
<!DOCTYPE html>

<html lang="en">
<head>
    <title>Functions</title>
    <script language="javascript"
type="text/javascript" src="attachment.
js"></script>
</head>
```

```
<body>
    <script language="javascript"
type="text/javascript">
        displaySport();
        displayStatistic();
    </script>
</body>
</html>
```

attachment.js:

```
function displaySport()
{
    document.write("Basketball and
Baseball... <br/> <br/>");
    document.write("Two A-W-E-S-O-M-E and
very P-O-P-U-L-A-R sports. <br/>");
}

function displayStatistic()
{
    statistic1 = 55;
    statistic2 = 56;
    document.write("<br/>Statistics show
" +statistic1+"% and "+statistic2+"%
respective audience patronage!");
}
```

Again, you are free to tweak the string values so that the output
will display your name and any numbers or figures you want
displayed. Have some fun while coding.

6.2 FUNCTIONS, PARAMETERS, AND RETURNS

One of the goals of writing functions in Javascript is to write functions that are both flexible and reusable. A good way to meet these goals is by creating functions that can both take parameters and return a value. In this section, we are going to discuss how to implement passing parameters and returning values.

In the previous section, we created a function called *displayPlayerScore*, which contained a variable that was set at 1000, then, we displayed the value of the variable.

This time, instead of having the value of the variable set inside the function, we will pass a value to the function and have that value used by a function.

For example, if we want to pass the value 14000 to the function, we would write:

```
displayPlayerScore(14000);
```

Now, the function *displayPlayerScore,* receives the value 14000 and assigns it to a variable. Let us call the variable *theScore;* we declare the complete function as:

```
function displayPlayerScore(theScore)
```

Oftentimes, you want to be able to manipulate the variable within the function and then return a new value to the function caller. For example, within the function you can write:

```
theScore += 1000;
```

This will add 1000 to the value that was passed to the function, known as *theScore*, then when called, it will return a new value as a result.

To clarify, the function is passed an initial value of 14000. The function assigns that value to the variable *theScore.*

```
function displayPlayerScore(theScore)
```

Within the function the code theScore += 1000; is run which increases the value of *theScore* to 15000.

The complete function would look like this:

```
function displayPlayerScore(theScore)
{
    theScore += 1000;
    document.write(theScore);
}
```

The function call would look like this:

```
displayPlayerScore(14000);
```

You may also pass multiple values to a function.

Suppose we have the values 100 and 17. In this example we will create a new function named *addTheseNumbers*, which will take the two values, add them together, and then display the sum.

To pass two values to a function, write the values within the function call inside the parentheses and then separate them with a comma:

```
addTheseNumbers(100,17);
```

The function declaration must also accommodate two variables. If we used *x* and *y* as the variables within the function, the function declaration might be written as:

```
function addTheseNumbers(x,y)
```

What we want to do now is take the values, add them together and output the result.

This is how the complete function should be structured:

```
function addTheseNumbers(x,y)
{
    document.write(x+y);
}
```

This function assigns the two values to the variables x and y, then outputs the result as the function is called.

Functions can also return a value when called. To demonstrate this, let's create a routine which will return the sum of x and y instead of displaying it with document.write().

The command that will make this possible is the **return** statement. Instead of using *document.write()*, we use *return*. The code is written as:

```
return(x+y);
```

Once the value is returned, the calling function must have a way of "catching" the returned value. The function call needs to be modified so that a variable will serve as recipient of the value being returned. The moment the value is returned by the function, it is then immediately assigned to a variable. The variable assignment for the function *addTheseNumbers* is sum and the function call should be written:

```
var sum = addTheseNumbers(100,17);
```

Remember, the right side of the assignment operator is always evaluated first; the two values, 100 and 17, will be passed to the function *addTheseNumbers* and the sum of the numbers will be returned and consequently, assigned to the variable *sum*.

Once the value is contained inside the variable, the variable output can then be generated.

> Keep in mind that when you are passing values to a function and returning values from a function, you always need a way of containing those values.

Code Listing: Calling Functions and Passing Values

```
<!DOCTYPE html>

<html>
<head>
    <title>Function Calls</title>
    <script language="javascript"
type="text/javascript" src="functionReturn.
js"></script>
</head>

<body>
    <script language="javascript"
type="text/javascript">
        //function calls
        displayGreeting();
        document.write("<br/>");

        displayPlayerScore(14000);
        document.write("<br/>");

        var sum=addTheseNumbers(12,17);
        document.write("<br/>");
        document.write(sum);
    </script>
</body>
</html>
Code Listing: functionReturn.js

function displayGreeting()
{
     document.write("Hey there, dude!");
}
```

```
function displayPlayerScore(theScore)
{
     //playerScore = 1000;
      theScore += 1000;   //theScore =
theScore + 1000;
document.write("<br/>Player score: " +
theScore);
}

function addTheseNumbers(x,y)
{
     //document.write(x+y);
      return (x+y);
}
```

> *To display the output, make sure your active window is the HTML*
> *document and not the .js file.*

This is the output of the above code:

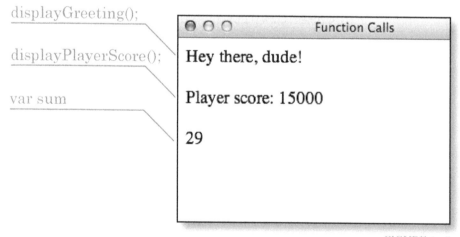

displayGreeting();

displayPlayerScore();

var sum

Function Calls

Hey there, dude!

Player score: 15000

29

FIGURE 6 - 5

136   *Javascript for Beginners*

QUESTIONS FOR REVIEW

1. How do you pass the value of a function?
   a. Put it in parentheses at the function call.
   b. Put it next to the function.
   c. Define it in the HTML.
   d. Play "pass the ball".

2. How do you return a value to a function call?
   a. return()
   b. sendback()
   c. functionReturn()
   d. returnValue()

3. What is needed to hold the value of the return command?
   a. A new function.
   b. A loop.
   c. A script.
   d. A variable.

6.3 CALLING FUNCTIONS FROM EVENTS

Javascript is often called an **event-driven language**. With Javascript, you can respond to events that the user causes in the user interface or events that occur naturally during the program's execution.

Four events will be covered in this section: **onclick, onload, onmouseover** and **onunload** and each of these events will be discussed accordingly.

Let's start with **onclick.** We're going to create a basic button in HTML that contains an onclick event. The onclick event will cause a Javascript function to execute when the button is clicked.

```
<input type="button" value="Press Me"
onclick="onButtonClick()"/>
```

Once this button is clicked, the function *onButtonClick()* will be executed. Now we need to create the actual function that will run when the button is clicked. We will write the function in <script> tags in the head of the document.

> When writing Javascript functions on a single page, it is always a good idea to keep them in the head of the document.

In this case, we are simply going to display a text alert that will say that the button has been pressed. The function is:

```
function onButtonClick()
    {
        alert("You have successfully
pressed the button!");

    }
```

When the code runs in the browser the following output is displayed:

FIGURE 6 - 6

Once the "Press Me" button is clicked, the function is called causing an "alert box" to appear on the webpage.

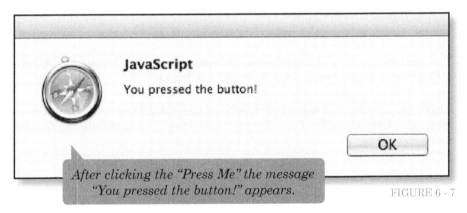

After clicking the "Press Me" the message "You pressed the button!" appears.

FIGURE 6 - 7

Following is the complete code listing for *onclick* event:

CODE LISTING: ONCLICK EVENT – WITH ALERT BOX

```
<!DOCTYPE html>

<html>
<head>
<title>onButtonClick</title>
    <script language="javascript"
type="text/javascript">
        function onButtonClick()
        {
            alert("You pressed the
button!");
        }
    </script>
</head>
<body>
<input type="button" value="Press Me!"
onclick="onButtonClick()">
</body>
</html>
```

The next event we will introduce is the **onload** event. This event triggers a function to be executed once the page has loaded.

There are a variety of ways to implement the onload event. A common method is to place *onload* inside the <body> tag. The complete tag for the *onload* event is:

```
<body onload="whenPageLoads()">
```

In the <body> tag shown, once the page is finished loading, the function *whenPageLoads()* will be executed. This function will give an *alert* message welcoming the user to the page.

Here the alert box was immediately displayed as soon as the page has loaded.

After clicking OK, the alert box clears.

FIGURE 6 - 8

FIGURE 6 - 9

Following is the complete code listing demonstrating *onload* event:

CODE LISTING: ONLOAD EVENT – WITH ALERT BOX

```
<!DOCTYPE html>

<html>
<head>
```

```
<title>onload Event</title>
<script language="javascript" type ="text/
javascript">
    function onLoad ()
    {
        alert ("Welcome To My Simple
Page!");
    }
</script>
</head>
<body onload="onLoad()">
Hello and Welcome Again!
</body>
</html>
```

Onload can be used in conjunction with *onclick*. You may have two separate functions for each event, like *whenPageLoads()* for the *onload* event and *onButtonClick()* for the *onclick* event. These functions are individually called as each event occurs during program execution. It is also possible to have multiple events pointing to the same function. This is more common if you have multiple buttons or other elements in your GUI that have a somewhat similar function.

In this next example, a "Welcome to my Page" alert box will be displayed once the page has loaded:

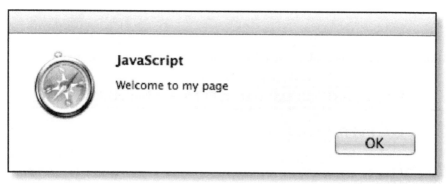

FIGURE 6 - 10

After clicking "OK", the alert box clears out, displaying the page with a "Press Me" button.

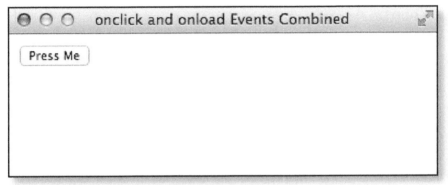

FIGURE 6 - 11

When the "Press Me" button is clicked, another alert box with the message "You have successfully pressed the button!" appears.

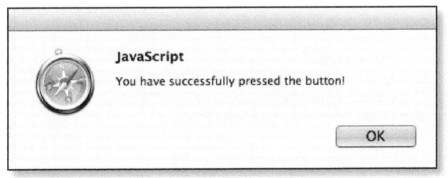

FIGURE 6 - 12

Clicking "OK" will clear out the alert box from the display.

Following is the complete code listing for *onclick* and *onload* events:

```html
<!DOCTYPE html>

<html>
<head>
    <title>onclick and onload Events
Combined</title>
</head>
<title>Events</title>
    <script language="javascript"
type="text/javascript">

    function whenPageLoads()
    {
        alert("Welcome to my page");
    }


        function onButtonClick()
    {
        alert("You have successfully
pressed the button!");
    }
    </script>
<body onload="whenPageLoads()">
  <input type="button" value="Press Me"
onclick="onButtonClick()"/>
</body>
</html>
```

Another event that can be used to trigger functions is **onmouseover**. This event triggers a function call when the user hovers the pointer over an HTML element displayed in the browser.

Let's tweak the previous example so that instead of clicking the mouse before the message "You have successfully pressed the button!" appears, a mouse hover will trigger display of the message window.

Following is the complete code listing for *onmouseover* event:

CODE LISTING: ONMOUSEOVER EVENT

```html
<!DOCTYPE html>

<html>
<head>
    <title>onmouseover Event</title>
    <script language="javascript"
type="text/javascript">

    function whenPageLoads()
    {
        alert("Welcome to my page");
    }
    function onMouseOver()
    {
        alert("You have successfully
hovered!");
    }
    </script>
</head>
<body onload="whenPageLoads()">
  <input type="button" value="Press Me"
onmouseover="onMouseOver()"/>
</body>
</html>
```

This is how the output will look when viewed in the browser:

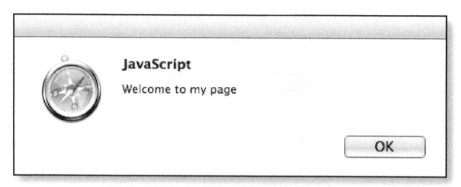

FIGURE 6 - 13

Click "OK". The message window will disappear and the "Press Me" button is now viewable. Hover the cursor over the button.

The second message window will appear by just hovering the cursor over the button and without clicking.

FIGURE 6 - 14

The last event we'll examine is the **onunload.** This event triggers a function call when the user exits a page. Let's add the onunload event in the previous example.

The complete code listing follows:

CODE LISTING: ONUNLOAD EVENT

```
<!DOCTYPE html>

<html>
<head>
    <title>onunload Event</title>
</head>
<title>Events</title>
    <script language="javascript"
type="text/javascript">

    function whenPageLoads()
    {
        alert("Welcome to my page!");
    }


        function onButtonClick()
    {
        alert("You have successfully
pressed the button!");
    }


        function whenPageUnloads()
    {
        alert("Bye! Please visit again!");
    }
    </script>
<body onload="whenPageLoads()" window.
onunload="whenPageUnloads()">
  <input type="button" value="Press Me"
onclick="onButtonClick()"/>
</body>
</html>
```

The output, when viewed in a browser, will be as follows for the onload event:

FIGURE 6 -15

and the onclick event:

FIGURE 6 - 16

However, screen capture of the onunload event is impossible because when the event occurs, the browser window essentially has been closed, and there is no existing context to show a dialog box.

QUESTIONS FOR REVIEW

1. How do you call a function from a user-generated event?
   a. Create a button and have the button associate an onclick event with the button.
   b. Embed the function in the HTML page.
   c. Create a loop that constantly loops the function.
   d. You can't.

2. What does the onload event do?
   a. Calls the function after the user closes the page.
   b. Calls the function when the user clicks the page.
   c. Calls the function after the page loads.
   d. Calls the function when the user puts their mouse over the page.

3. What is the difference between the events onmouseover and onclick?
   a. onmouseover triggers an event when the web element is clicked, while onclick triggers the event when hovered on.
   b. onmouseover triggers an event when the web element is hovered on, while onclick triggers the event when clicked.
   c. They both trigger an event when the page is loaded.
   d. They both trigger an event when the page is unloaded.

CHAPTER 6 LAB EXERCISE

1) Greetings

Write a program routine that will display a greeting corresponding to the language that was clicked. The greetings will be in four languages and are as follows:

English= Hello! How are you?
Spanish= Hola! Como estas?
Hebrew= Shalom!
French= Bonjour!

Create a basic HTML5 document structure.

Place a <script> element in the document head with the appropriate attributes and values so you can add Javascript code.

```
<head>
<title>Chapter 6 Lab Exercise' 1</title>
<script language="javascript" type="text/
javascript">
</script>
</head>
```

In the script element you just created, include the following functions:

```
English()
Spanish()
Hebrew()
French()

<title>Chapter 6 Lab Exercise 1</title>
<script language="javascript" type="text/
javascript">
function English()
{}
function Spanish()
{}
function Hebrew()
{}
function French()
{}
</script>
```

Using the *onclick* event, add the necessary attributes in creating each of the buttons' <input> elements.

Using an alert box, complete the code so that each of the previous greetings are displayed, one at a time, depending on the language button that was clicked.

Save your completed file. Test and make sure that it works correctly.

2A) Some Arithmetic

Write a program that will add, subtract, multiply, or divide two integers, 25 and 260 for example, when the corresponding button for the arithmetic operation is clicked.

Create a new basic HTML5 document.

In the document heading, include Javascript <script> tags accordingly.

```
<head>
<title>Chapter 6 Lab Exercise Solution 2A</title>
<script language="javascript" type="text/javascript">
</script>
</head>
```

Include the functions: *add (), subtract (), multiply (), and divide ()* in the script element in the document head.

```
<script language="javascript" type="text/javascript">
function add(x,y)
{
document.write(x + "+" + y + "=" + (x+y));
}
function subtract(x,y)
{
document.write(x + "-" + y + "=" + (x-y));
}
function multiply(x,y)
{
document.write(x + "*" + y + "=" + (x*y));
}
function divide(x,y)
{
document.write(x + "/" + y + "=" + (x/y));
}
</script>
```

Create four buttons labeled "add", "subtract", "multiply" and "divide". Call each of the arithmetic operation functions when the *onclick* event button is clicked.

```
<body>
<input type="button" value="Add"
onclick="add(25,60)"/>
<input type="button" value="Subtract"
onclick="subtract(25,60)"/>
<input type="button" value="Multiply"
onclick="multiply(25,60)"/>
<input type="button" value="Divide"
onclick="divide(25,60)"/>
```

When the *onclick* event is called, each function should display the resulting value for adding, subtracting, multiplying or dividing the integers.

2B) Some Arithmetic Using One Function

Save and test. Once the code is already working, improve the program code so that the same functionalities are accomplished with only one function in the document heading called *mathProb()*. Three parameters must be "passed" to this function—the two integers and any one of the symbols: +, -, * or / that corresponds to the mathematical function to be performed.

> *When you pass the symbol to the function as a parameter, enclose it within single quotes, not double quotes. The onclick attribute will already be surrounded with double quotes—so if you need to use quotes while already within double quotes, use single quotes.*

3) Modify Chapter Lab Exercise 2A

Modify chapter 6 lab exercise 2A so that the program will let the user choose the arithmetic operation to be performed, then input two random integers (one after the other) and then display the result.

4) Modify Chapter Lab Exercise 2B

Modify chapter 6 lab exercise 2B so that the program will accept two random integers, the arithmetic operation desired: "+" sign for addition, "-" sign for subtraction, "*" sign for multiplication and "/" for division then display the result.

LAB EXERCISE SOLUTIONS

Greetings

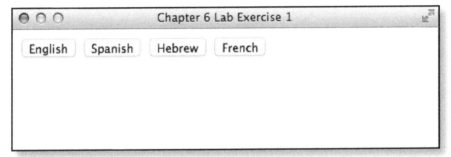

FIGURE 6 - 17

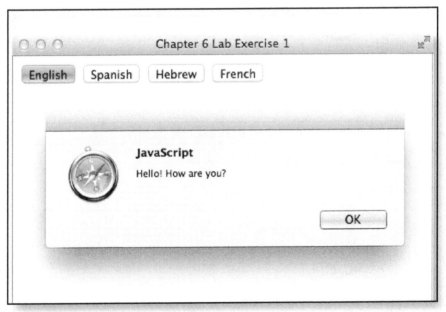

FIGURE 6 - 18

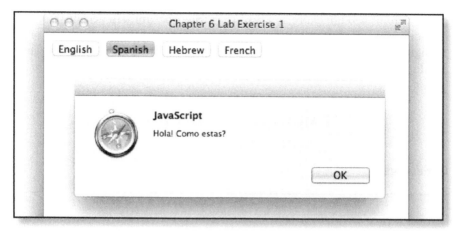

FIGURE 6 - 19

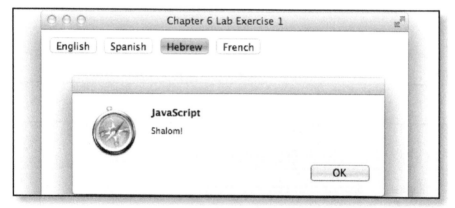

FIGURE 6 - 20

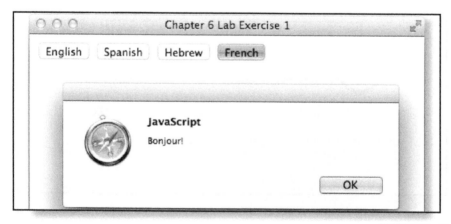

FIGURE 6 - 21

CODE LISTING: GREETINGS

```html
<!DOCTYPE html>

<html>
<head>
    <title>Chapter 6 Lab Exercise 1</title>
    <script language="javascript"
type="text/javascript">
        function English()
        {
            alert("Hello! How are you?");
        }
        function Spanish()
        {
            alert("Hola! Como estas?");
        }
        function Hebrew()
        {
            alert("Shalom!");
        }
        function French()
        {
            alert("Bonjour!");
        }
    </script>
</head>

<body>
    <input type="button" value="English"
onclick="English()"/>
    <input type="button" value="Spanish"
onclick="Spanish()"/>
    <input type="button" value="Hebrew"
onclick="Hebrew()"/>
    <input type="button" value="French"
```

```
        onclick="French()"/>
    </script>
</body>
</html>
```

2A) Some Arithmetic

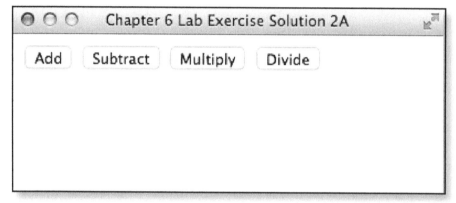

FIGURE 6 - 22

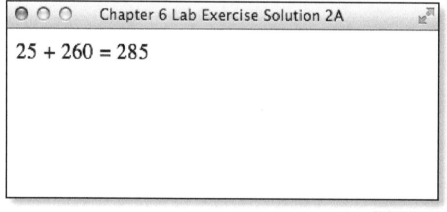

FIGURE 6 - 23

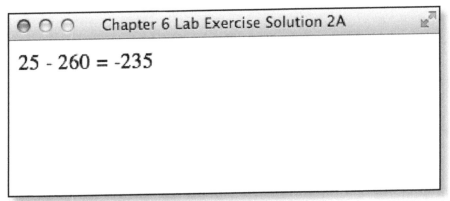

FIGURE 6 - 24

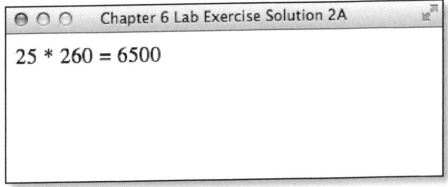

FIGURE 6 - 25

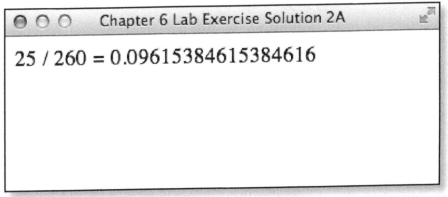

FIGURE 6 - 26

CODE LISTING: SOME ARITHMETIC

```
<!DOCTYPE html>

<html>
<head>
    <title>Chapter 6 Lab Exercise Solution
2A</title>
    <script language="javascript"
type="text/javascript">
        function add(x,y)
        {
            document.write(x + " + " + y +
" = " + (x+y));
        }
        function subtract(x,y)
        {
            document.write(x + " - " + y +
" = "  + (x-y));
        }
        function multiply(x,y)
        {
            document.write(x + " * " + y +
" = " + (x*y));
        }
        function divide(x,y)
        {
            document.write(x + " / " + y +
" = " + (x/y));
        }
    </script>
</head>
<body>
    <input type="button" value="Add"
onclick="add(25,260)"/>
    <input type="button" value="Subtract"
```

```
onclick="subtract(25,260)" />
    <input type="button" value ="Multiply"
onclick="multiply(25,260)"/>
    <input type="button" value="Divide"
onclick="divide(25,260)"/>
</body>
</html>
```

2B) Some arithmetic using the function *mathProb()*

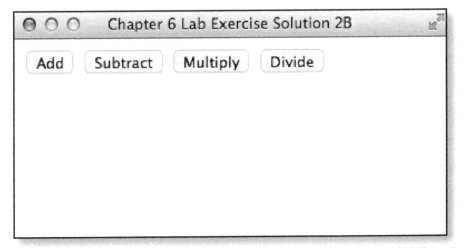

FIGURE 6 - 27

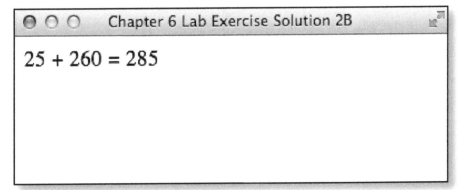

FIGURE 6 - 28

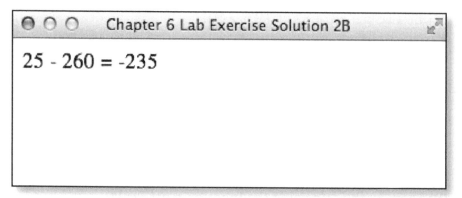

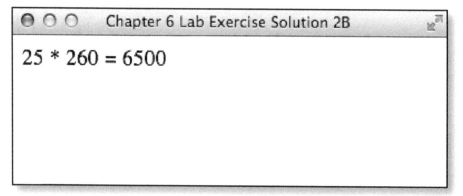

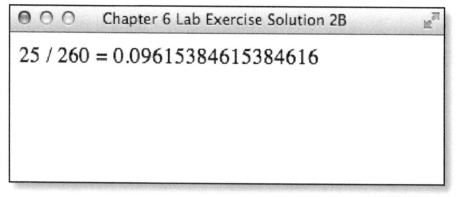

CODE LISTING: SOME ARITHMETIC USING THE FUNCTION *MATHPROB()*

```
<!DOCTYPE html>

<head>
    <title>Chapter 6 Lab Exercise Solution
2A</title>
    <script language="javascript"
type="text/javascript">
        function mathProb(x,y,symbol)
        {
            switch(symbol)
            {
                case "+":
                    document.write(x + " +
" + y + " = " + (x+y));
                    break;
                case "-":
                    document.write(x + " -
" + y + " = " + (x-y));
                    break;
                case "*":
                    document.write(x + " *
" + y + " = " + (x*y));
                    break;
                case "/":
                    document.write(x + " /
" + y + " = " + (x/y));
            }
        }

    </script>
</head>
<body>
    <input type="button" value="add"
```

```
onclick="mathProb(25,260,'+')"/>
    <input type="button" value="subtract"
onclick="mathProb(25,260,'-')" />
    <input type="button" value ="multiply"
onclick="mathProb(25,260,'*')"/>
    <input type="button" value="divide"
onclick="mathProb(25,260,'/')"/>
</body>
</html>
```

3) Modified Lab Exercise 2A

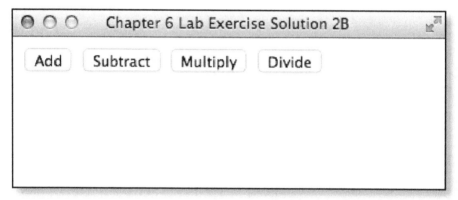

FIGURE 6 - 32

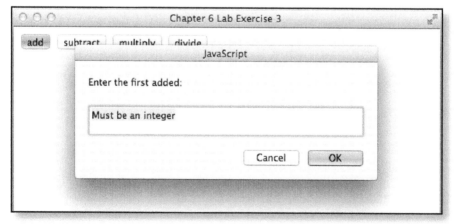

FIGURE 6 - 33

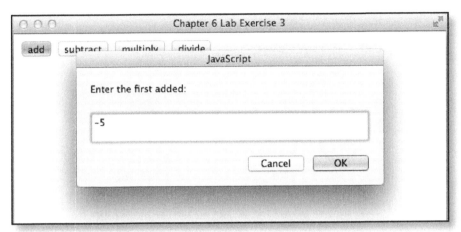

FIGURE 6 - 34

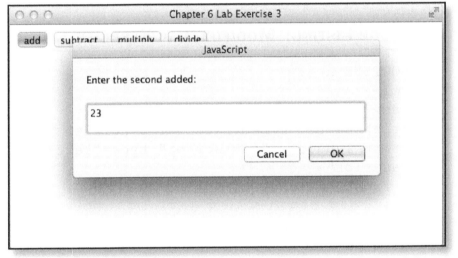

FIGURE 6 - 35

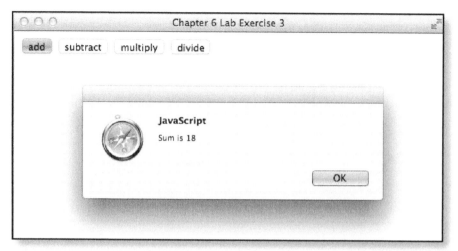

FIGURE 6 - 36

CODE LISTING: MODIFIED LAB EXERCISE 2A

```
<!DOCTYPE html>
<html>
<head>
<title>Chapter 6 Lab Exercise 3</title>
<script language="javascript" type="text/
javascript">
    function add()
    {
        var x = parseInt(prompt("Enter the
first addend:" , "Must be an integer"));
        var y = parseInt(prompt("Enter the
second addend:" , "Must be an integer"));
        var sum = x+y;
        alert("Sum is " + sum);
    }
    function subtract(x,y)
    {
        x = parseInt(prompt("Enter the
minuend:" , "Must be an integer"));
        y = parseInt(prompt("Enter the
```

```
subtrahend:" , "Must be an integer"));
      var difference = x-y;
      alert("Difference is " +
difference);
    }
    function multiply(x,y)
    {
        x = parseInt(prompt("Enter the
multiplicand" , "Must be an integer"));
        y = parseInt(prompt("Enter the
multiplier" , "Must be an integer"));
      var product = x*y;
      alert("Product is " + product);
    }
    function divide(x,y)
    {
        x = parseInt(prompt("Enter the
dividend: " , "Must be an integer"));
        y = parseInt(prompt("Enter the
divisor: " , "Must be an integer and not
equal to 0"));
      var quotient = x/y;
      alert("Quotient is " + quotient);
    }
</script>
</head>
<body>
    <input type="button" value="add"
onclick="add()"/>
    <input type="button" value="subtract"
onclick="subtract()" />
    <input type="button" value="multiply"
onclick="multiply()"/>
    <input type="button" value="divide"
onclick="divide()"/>
</body>
</html>
```

4) Modified Lab Exercise 2B

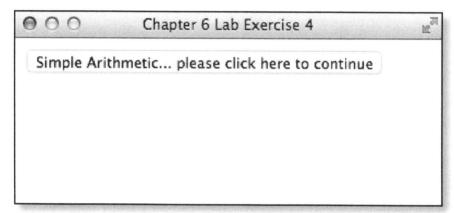

FIGURE 6 - 37

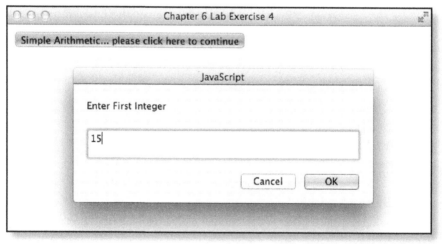

FIGURE 6 - 38

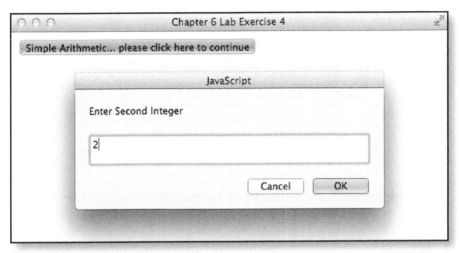

FIGURE 6 - 39

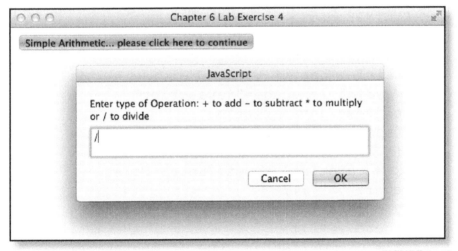

FIGURE 6 - 40

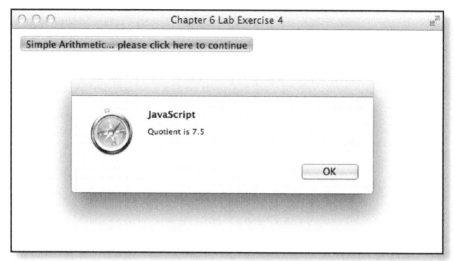

FIGURE 6 - 41

CODE LISTING: MODIFIED CHAPTER LAB EXERCISE 2B

```
<!DOCTYPE html>
<html>
   <head>
   <title>Chapter 6 Lab Exercise 4</title>
   <script language="javascript"
type="text/javascript">
   function mathProb(x,y,z)
   {
   x = parseInt(prompt("Enter First
Integer" , ""));
   y = parseInt(prompt("Enter Second
Integer" , ""));
   z = prompt("Enter type of Operation: +
to add - to subtract * to multiply or / to
divide" , "");

   if (z == "+")
   {
```

```
var sum = x+y;
alert("Sum is " + sum);
}
else if (z == "-")
{
var difference = x-y;
alert("Difference is " + difference);
}
else if (z == "*")
{
var product = x*y;
alert("Product is " + product);
}
else if (z == "/")
{
var quotient = x/y;
alert("Quotient is " + quotient);
}
}
</script>
</head>
<body>
<input type="button" value="Simple
Arithmetic... please click here to continue"
onclick="mathProb()" />

</body>
</html>
```

CHAPTER 6 SUMMARY

In Chapter 6, we discussed functions in Javascript. Functions are blocks of code that can be called from a page and reused as many times as needed. You learned how to create functions within a page and attach them in a separate file, which allowed greater flexibility in using functions across multiple web pages.

You also learned how to pass values to a function and return values to the function caller. We discussed how to manipulate the values that were sent to the function and return the new values.

We also covered how to use events to trigger functions. Here, we taught how to use the *onclick, onload, onmouseover* and *onunload* events.

In the next chapter, we will be focusing on creating and manipulating arrays.

CHAPTER 7

WORKING WITH ARRAYS

CHAPTER OBJECTIVES:

- You will be able to create and declare arrays.
- You will learn how to use the for-loop to index arrays.
- You will be able to manipulate arrays via the push and pop functions.
- You will learn how to sort and splice arrays.

7.1 DECLARING ARRAYS

In chapter 7 we will be discussing arrays. Arrays are objects that are capable of holding a series of values all at one time. For example, if you need to keep a list of all the products a company offers within one variable, an array may contain all these as values or a series of values.

Creating an array is fairly straightforward. There are three methods of creating arrays in Javascript.

 The first one is the **standard method**, which is accomplished by creating a variable and assigning a new **Array()** object to the variable. This process is known as instantiation of an array object. For example:

```
var firstNames = new Array();
```

Populating the standard array is done by writing the variable name followed by the array index and using the assignment operator as you would with a variable. For example:

```
firstNames[0]= "John";
firstNames[1]= "Mary";
firstNames[2]= "Jane";
firstNames[3]= "Sam";
firstNames[4]= "Johnny";
```

The **array index** is the position of the value in the array. In the previous example, they are the numbers enclosed in the square brackets:
[0], [1], [2], [3], [4].

Arrays always start with the position 0; therefore when populating your array, you must always start with the "0" index. A common error developers make when working with Arrays is known as the "one-off error." Because the first member of the array is in index 0 and the second member is in index 1, it is common for programmers to be "one off" when selecting an index from the array.

Following is the HTML code listing that shows the standard assignment for arrays. The array variable *firstNames* has been assigned five values:

```html
<html>
<head>
<title>
</title>
</head>
<body>
    <script language="javascript"
type="text/javascript">
    var firstNames = new Array();
    firstNames[0] = "John";
    firstNames[1] = "Mary";
    firstNames[2] = "Jane";
    firstNames[3] = "Sam";
    firstNames[4] = "Johnny";
    </script>
</body>
</html>
```

Another way of creating an array is by using the **condensed method**. The condensed method is simply a truncated way of assigning values to the array. Instead of assigning values individually, we write out the members of the array within the instantiation, putting the array objects all in the same line of code as follows:

```
<html>
<head>
<title>
</title>
</head>
<body>
    <script language="javascript"
type="text/javascript">

    var animals = new Array( "dog", "cat",
"mouse", "hamster", "toad");
    </script>
</body>
</html>
```

> **Even though this method doesn't assign numbers to the list of arrays, you should know that the first array is always index number *zero* by default.**

var animals = new Array("dog", "cat", "mouse", "hamster", "toad");

Index Numbers: [0] [1] [2] [3] [4]

The third and final method of creating an array is the **literal array method**. In this method, an array is created by declaring a variable and setting the values in square brackets separated by commas. The difference lies in the instantiation where the new variable and data type declaration "new Array" are no longer included in the code:

```
<html>
<head>
<title>
</title>
</head>
<body>
    <script language="javascript"
type="text/javascript">
    var companies = ["Apple", "Google",
"Cnet", "Udemy", "GE"];
```

> **The same index numbering scheme applies to this method as well.**

```
        </script>
    </body>
    </html>
```

var companies = ["Apple", "Google", "Cnet", "Udemy", "GE"];

Index Numbers: [0]   [1]   [2]   [3]   [4]

These three methods work essentially the same way and the results are the same. Once the array is created the Javascript interpreter within the browser makes no distinction on how the array was created. In the three examples above, all of the arrays have five members that can be accessed by their index number. The dialogue box "alert" can be used to display any member of the array.

CODE LISTING: STANDARD METHOD
ARRAY DECLARATION
DISPLAY ARRAY MEMBER

```
<!DOCTYPE html>

<html>
<head>
    <title>Standard Array</title>
</head>
<body>
    <script language="javascript"
type="text/javascript">
        var firstNames = new Array();
            firstNames[0] = "John";
            firstNames[1] = "Mary";
            firstNames[2] = "Jane";
            firstNames[3] = "Sam";
            firstNames[4] = "Johnny";
            alert(firstNames[3]);
```

```
    </script>
</body>
</html>
```

This is how the output looks when viewed in the browser:

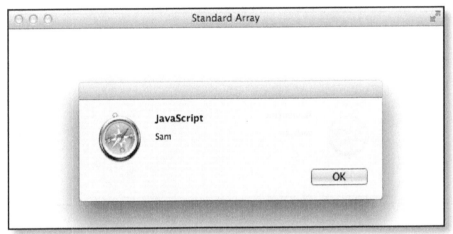

FIGURE 7 - 1

CODE LISTING: CONDENSED METHOD

```
<!DOCTYPE html>

<html>
<head>
    <title>Condensed Array</title>
</head>

<body>
    <script language="javascript"
type="text/javascript">
var animals = new Array("dog", "cat",
"mouse", "hamster", "toad");
```

```
alert(animals[3]);
    </script>
</body>
</html>
```

This is how the output looks when viewed in the browser:

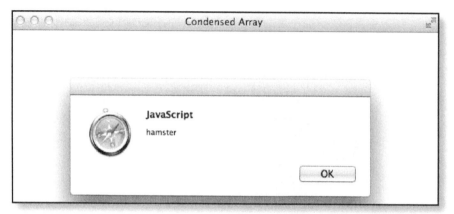

FIGURE 7 - 2

CODE LISTING: LITERAL METHOD

```
<!DOCTYPE html>

<html>
<head>
    <title>Literal Array</title>
</head>

<body>
    <script language="javascript"
type="text/javascript">
        var companies = ["Apple", "Google",
"Cnet", "Udemy", "GE"];

        alert(companies[3]);
    </script>
```

```
</body>
</html>
```

This is how the output looks when viewed in the browser:

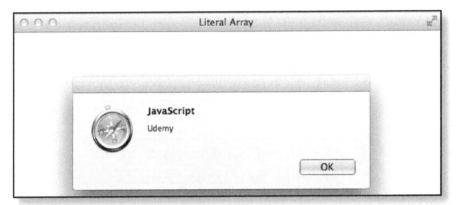

FIGURE 7 - 3

It may be confusing at first that you are writing three (3) in the square brackets yet you are accessing the fourth item in the list, but you will get used to the referencing with frequent use of arrays.

If you want to access the members of the array sequentially, the best method to use is the loop. Javascript arrays have a **length property**. The length property returns the number of members of an array. Remember that in most cases this will be one *more* than the highest index of the array, since all arrays are zero indexed in Javascript.

For example, let's say you want to access the length of the array *firstNames()*. To do this, we write the array variable name followed by a period then by the property length:

```
firstNames.length
```

To use the property within the loop, we have to establish the loop conditional where the condition compares the value with the array's length. The code listing should look like this:

```
for (var i = 0; i < firstNames.length; i++);
```

```
{
document.write (firstNames[i]);
document.write ("<br/>);
}
```

In this loop, the variable *i* is initially set to zero and as long as that number is less than than the length of *firstNames*, the loop executes. The loop will then output all the array indices values and stop once the content of the last index has been displayed or sent out.

Following is the code listing that will show how to display all index values of an array:

CODE LISTING: STANDARD ARRAY— DISPLAY ALL INDEX VALUES

```
<!DOCTYPE html>

<html>
<head>
    <title>Standard Array</title>
</head>
<body>
    <script language="javascript"
type="text/javascript">
var firstNames = new Array();
firstNames[0] = "John";
firstNames[1] = "Mary";
firstNames[2] = "Jane";
firstNames[3] = "Sam";
firstNames[4] = "Johnny";

for(var i=0; i<firstNames.length; i++)
{
document.write (firstNames[i]);
document.write ("<br/>");
}
```

```
    </script>
  </body>
  </html>
```

This is how the output of the previous code listing will look when viewed in the browser:

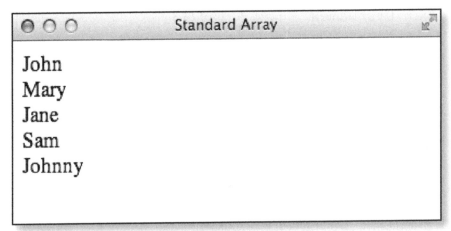

FIGURE 7 - 4

You can also change the value of an index in an array after it has been instantiated. To do this, you need to indicate the index location you wish to change and declare the new value. Here's the code:

```
firstNames[0]= "Herbert";
```

Insert the previous code inside another for-loop and see how the first array element changes value.

The complete code listing now becomes:

CODE LISTING: STANDARD ARRAY WITH FOR-LOOP

```
<!DOCTYPE html>

<html>
<head>
```

```
    <title>Standard Array with For-Loop</
title>
</head>
<body>
    <script language="javascript"
type="text/javascript">

var firstNames = new Array();
firstNames[0] = "John";
firstNames[1] = "Mary";
firstNames[2] = "Jane";
firstNames[3] = "Sam";
firstNames[4] = "Johnny";

// Display original firstNames[0]

for(var i=0; i<firstNames.length; i++)
{
document.write (firstNames[i]);
document.write ("<br/>");
}
// Display a new value for firstNames[0]

firstNames[0] = "Herbert";

for(var i=0; i<firstNames.length; i++)
{
document.write (firstNames[i]);
document.write ("<br/>");
}
    </script>
</body>
</html>
```

This is how the output will look when viewed in the browser:

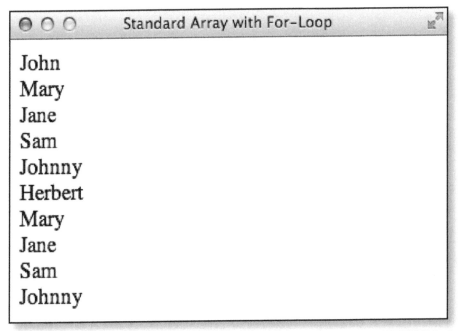

FIGURE 7 - 5

Notice how the value for *index [0]* has changed to "Herbert" from "John" while the rest of the array members were left unchanged.

1. What are arrays?
   a. Variables that can hold more than one value at a time.
   b. Loops that can loop more than one variable at a time.
   c. Loops that are used in Javascript.
   d. Functions that can hold more than one value at a time.

2. What do you call the process of creating an array?
   a. Declaration of an array.
   b. Referencing an array.
   c. Assigning an array.
   d. Instantiation of an array.

3. In the condensed array method, where do you write the assigned values?
   a. On separate lines.
   b. On the same line as the array.
   c. In a new Javascript file.
   d. In a new variable.

4. How do you access all the members of an array?
   a. By using a function.
   b. By creating a new array.
   c. By using a loop.
   d. By passing the data of the function to the variable.

7.2 MANIPULATING ARRAYS

As you work with arrays you'll frequently find it necessary to manipulate the data stored within the array. In Javascript, as with most contemporary programming languages, an array is an object. Language objects have properties that describe the object—like *length*—and they have methods (sometimes also called functions—just to confuse you) that allow you to manipulate the object. In this section we'll look at some of the available properties and methods of the array object.

Take a look at the following example. We have an array that contains 10 values representing test grades. For simplicity, we'll use the variable name *grades*. The values contained by the variable *grades* are as follows: 85, 92, 70, 63, 55, 92, 88, 77, 91, and 91, for a total of 10 array members.

Let's see what happens when we attempt to display the 12th member of the array—which would be located in the non-existent 11th index—expressed in code as grades[11].

Type the following code listing in your editor and view the output.

CODE LISTING: LITERAL ARRAY DISPLAYING AN OBJECT IN THE ARRAY—OBJECT OUT OF RANGE

```
<!DOCTYPE html>

<html>
<head>
    <title>Literal Array</title>
</head>
<body>
<script language="javascript" type="text/
javascript">
var grades = [85, 92, 70, 63, 55, 92, 88,
77, 91, 91]
document.write (grades[11]);
</script>
```

```
</body>
</html>
```

Following is the expected output:

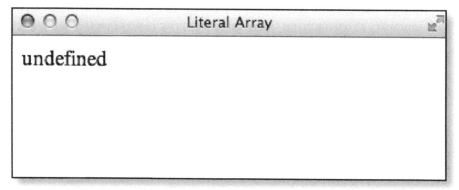

FIGURE 7 - 6

The code yielded an undefined message since a 12th member (that is, *grades[11]*) of the array does not exist. This is called a logical error. It is the kind of error where the program runs but does not display the expected result. Errors of this type cannot be easily found using traditional syntax checkers. Therefore, you must employ care in analysis of program logic when identifying and working with arrays and their data.

We will now change

```
document.write (grades[11]);
```

to:

```
document.write (grades[9]);
```

so that it will display the 10th member of the array. The updated code listing will now be:

CODE LISTING: LITERAL ARRAY DISPLAYING AN OBJECT IN THE ARRAY—OBJECT WITHIN RANGE

```
<!DOCTYPE html>

<html>
<head>
    <title>Literal Array</title>
</head>
<body>
<script language="javascript" type="text/
javascript">
var grades = [85, 92, 70, 63, 55, 92, 88,
77, 91, 91]
document.write (grades[9]);
</script>
</body>
</html>
```

The output should be:

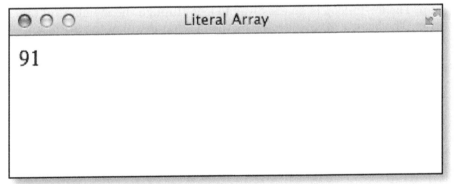

FIGURE 7 - 7

The number of members or values of the array can also be displayed. This is done by appending the length property in the variable *grades* and that is, **grades.length.** The Javascript elements will be as follows:

```
<script language="javascript" type="text/
javascript">
var grades = [85, 92, 70, 63, 55, 92, 88,
77, 91, 91]
    document.write (grades[9]);
document.write ("</br>" + grades.length);

    for (x in grades)
        {
    document.write("Iteration:" + grades);

document.write("</br>" + grades[x] + "</
br>");
        }
</script>
```

Remember that the length is always greater by 1
than the last index number declared in the array.

Let us now do an iteration of the members of the array using **for-in-
loop**. The for-in-loop is an easy way to loop through the members of the
array. The beauty of this looping method is that it will automatically
loop through each member of the array just based on its length property
without needing to know what the actual length of the array is. The
length is used implicitly without being explicitly stated. (Mention that
tonight at the dinner table and see what kind of reaction you get...)

We'll write the code that will display the length of the *array* grades and
its iteration number on the next line; this will happen for each of the
array members successively and on separate lines. The code listing is as
follows:

CODE LISTING: FOR-IN-LOOP

```
<!DOCTYPE html>

<html>
<head>
    <title>Literal Array For-In-Loop</
title>
</head>

<body>
    <script language="javascript"
type="text/javascript">
        var grades = [85,92,70,63, 55,
92,88,77,91,91];
        //Display array length
        document.write ("Array length: " +
grades.length + "<br/>");
        //Display Iteration then the grade
        for(x in grades)
        {
            document.write ("Iteration: " +
x + "<br/>");
            document.write (grades[x] +
"<br/>");
        }
    </script>
</body>
</html>
```

The output of the presented code will be:

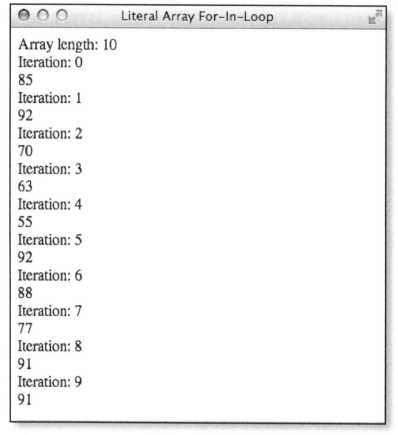

Array length: 10
Iteration: 0
85
Iteration: 1
92
Iteration: 2
70
Iteration: 3
63
Iteration: 4
55
Iteration: 5
92
Iteration: 6
88
Iteration: 7
77
Iteration: 8
91
Iteration: 9
91

FIGURE 7 - 8

Let's take a look at some of the methods you can use with Javascript array objects.

If you want a more complete reference for the array object, visit
http://www.w3schools.com/jsref/jsref_obj_array.asp
which contains a comprehensive listing of properties and methods.

We'll take a look at the **push** method first. *Push* is a function that adds new indexes and data to the end of the array and then returns the new length. The syntax for implementing *push*, using the same array *grades*, is as follows:

Push

```
grades.push(new value 1, new value 2, ...);
```

Modifying the Javascript element from the previous code, we will have:

```
<script language="javascript" type="text/
javascript">
var grades = [85,92,70,63, 55,
92,88,77,91,91];
document.write ("Array length: " + grades.
length + "<br/>");
grades.push(100,63);

for(x in grades)
{
document.write ("Iteration " + x + ": ");
document.write (grades[x] + "<br/>");
}
</script>
```

The values 100 and 63 found inside the parentheses associated with the push method are added to the end of the array in new indexes.

We can now modify the code in the previous example, adding the two new values to the array and return the new array length. The new code listing is as follows:

CODE LISTING: LITERAL ARRAY IN FOR-IN-LOOP WITH PUSH

```
<!DOCTYPE html>

<html>
<head>
    <title>Literal Array For-In-loop with
Push</title>
</head>

<body>
```

```
<script language="javascript"
type="text/javascript">
    var grades = [85,92,70,63, 55,
92,88,77,91,91];
    //Display array length.
    document.write ("Array length: " +
grades.length + "<br/>");
    grades.push(100,63);
    //Display iteration and grades.
    for(x in grades)
    {
        document.write ("Iteration " +
x + ": ");
        document.write (grades[x] +
"<br/>");
    }

     document.write ("<br/> Array
length after PUSH: " + grades.length +
"<br/>");
    </script>
</body>
</html>
```

The output will look like this:

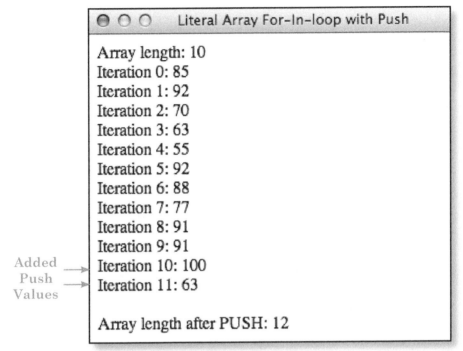

Array length: 10
Iteration 0: 85
Iteration 1: 92
Iteration 2: 70
Iteration 3: 63
Iteration 4: 55
Iteration 5: 92
Iteration 6: 88
Iteration 7: 77
Iteration 8: 91
Iteration 9: 91
Added Push Values → Iteration 10: 100
→ Iteration 11: 63

Array length after PUSH: 12

FIGURE 7 - 9

Notice the two new values—100 and 63, added at the end of the list—and the new array length at the bottom that indicates 12.

Closely related to the *push* method is another function called **pop**. *Pop* simply removes the last element of the array.

In the previous example, if the code *grades.push(100, 63)* added 100 and 63 to the bottom list of the array (63 being the last entry), appending the instruction *grades.pop()* right after *grades.push(100, 63)* will bump off 63 from the array list, leaving 100 as the last entry and leaving "63" in a temporary memory storage, awaiting a "return".

Assigning the popped object to a declared variable will catch the awaiting value which later may be reused for another purpose or routine.

To demonstrate how that works in the actual code, let us look at the following command lines:

```
grades.push(100, 63);
```

will add 100 and 63 in the *grades* array.

Writing the *pop* instruction will pop "63" out of the array, and assign it to a variable. This code can be written as:

```
var popped = grades.pop();
```

The variable *popped* will now hold the value "63" after it is bumped off of the array list.

The complete Javascript code below demonstrates the use of *pop* more completely:

CODE LISTING: LITERAL ARRAY FOR-IN-LOOP WITH PUSH AND POP

```
<!DOCTYPE html>
<html>
<head>
    <title>Literal Array For-In-loop with
Push and Pop</title>
</head>

<body>
    <script language="javascript"
type="text/javascript">
var grades = [85,92,70,63, 55,
92,88,77,91,91];
document.write ("Initial Array length: " +
grades.length + "<br/>");
grades.push(100,63);

for(x in grades)
        {
```

```
            document.write ("Iteration " +
x + ": ");
            document.write (grades[x] +
"<br/>");
        }
            document.write ("<br/> Array
length after PUSH: " + grades.length +
"<br/>");
var popped = grades.pop();
document.write ("<br/> The object POPped is
" + popped +"<br/>");
document.write ("<br/> Array length after
POP: " + grades.length + "<br/>");

document.write ("<br/> Iteration after POP:
" + "<br/><br/>");
for(x in grades)
        {
            document.write ("Iteration " +
x + ": ");
            document.write (grades[x] +
"<br/>");
        }
    </script>
</body>
</html>
```

The function **document.write (popped)** displays the value popped off the array object: "63".

The following is the code output:

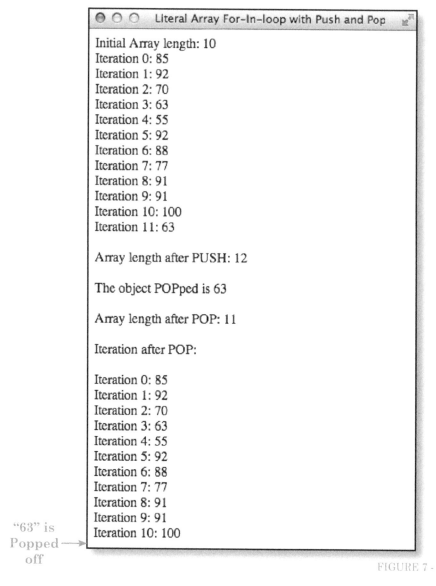

```
●  ○  ○    Literal Array For-In-loop with Push and Pop

Initial Array length: 10
Iteration 0: 85
Iteration 1: 92
Iteration 2: 70
Iteration 3: 63
Iteration 4: 55
Iteration 5: 92
Iteration 6: 88
Iteration 7: 77
Iteration 8: 91
Iteration 9: 91
Iteration 10: 100
Iteration 11: 63

Array length after PUSH: 12

The object POPped is 63

Array length after POP: 11

Iteration after POP:

Iteration 0: 85
Iteration 1: 92
Iteration 2: 70
Iteration 3: 63
Iteration 4: 55
Iteration 5: 92
Iteration 6: 88
Iteration 7: 77
Iteration 8: 91
Iteration 9: 91
Iteration 10: 100
```

"63" is
Popped →
off

FIGURE 7 - 10

Another method (or function) we can use to manipulate the array data is
sort. The *sort* array function sorts the members of the array
alphabetically.

Sort

Let's start a new array called *names* and declare the same using the
literal method.

```
var names = ["Phil", "Bob", "Tom", "Oscar",
"Jane"]
```

The array variable assigned is *names*. This array contains five elements. Using the *sort* function, we will sort and display the array objects alphabetically.

The syntax for the *sort* function is:

```
names.sort();
```

Let's now write the complete program code to sort the array, *names( )*.

```
<!DOCTYPE html>

<html>
<head>
    <title>Array: Names</title>
</head>
<body>
    <script language="javascript"
type="text/javascript">
        // Create and declare the array
        var names = ["Phil", "Bob", "Tom",
"Oscar", "Mary", "Jane"];
        //Sort the array
        names.sort();
        //Display the array list
        for (var y = 0; y < names.
length;y++)
        {
            document.write(names[y] +
"<br/>");
        }
    </script>
</body>
</html>
```

The final array method we will discuss is **splice**. *Splice* allows removal of objects or array members anywhere within the array. Using this function, the index location of the first object and number of items to be removed must be indicated. The syntax for use with the *splice* function is:

Splice

```
arrayName.splice(index number of first item to be
removed, number of objects to be removed);
```

Example:

```
placesToVisit.splice(0, 2);
```

The example shown will access the array named *placesToVisit* and will perform the function *splice* on the first and second element of the array: *placesToVisit[0]* and *placesToVisit[1]*.

The chapter lab exercise will demonstrate the combined use of these array methods. It is a good idea to try practicing with your own array data so you can get used to manipulating arrays.

CHAPTER 7 LAB EXERCISE

1) Create a new basic HTML document and insert Javascript tags.

2) Create an array called *placesToVisit* using any of the three methods discussed. Populate the array with the names of at least five places you'd like to visit.

3) Using a for-loop, loop through the array displaying the name of each place using *document.write()*.

4) Add the city "Boise" at the end of the array.

5) Create a loop that displays the array through the function *outputArray()*. Make sure your function will accept a single parameter called *theArray*.

6) Call the function *outputArray()* and pass the array *placesToVisit*.

7) In the body of the HTML, call the *outputArray()* function again to output the parameter, *theArray* after the changes are made.

8) Remove the first two members of the array through the *splice* function. The correct syntax for the function is:

```
placesToVisit.splice(0, 2);
```

9) Call the *outputArray()* function and instruct that the array be displayed again showing the changes made.

10) Sort the array alphabetically.

11) Using the function created, display the array for the last time.

12) Save and test your code. View the output in your browser.

This is how your output should look when viewed in the browser:

Mt. Fuji
Great Wall
Lake Superior
Victoria Falls
Chocolate Hills
Mt. Pinatubo
Boracay
Big Ben
North Pole
Boise

Lake Superior
Victoria Falls
Chocolate Hills
Mt. Pinatubo
Boracay
Big Ben
North Pole
Boise

Big Ben
Boise
Boracay
Chocolate Hills
Lake Superior
Mt. Pinatubo
North Pole
Victoria Falls

FIGURE 7 - 11

CODE LISTING: CHAPTER LAB EXERCISE SOLUTION

```
<html>
<head>
<title>Chapter Lab Exercise</title>
    <script language="javascript"
type="text/javascript">
        function outputArray(theArray)
        {
            for(x in placesToVisit)
            {
            document.write(placesToVisit[x]
+ "</br>");
            }
        }
    </script>
</head>
<body>
    <script language="javascript"
type="text/javascript">
        var placesToVisit = ["Mt. Fuji",
"Great Wall", "Lake Superior", "Victoria
Falls", "Chocolate Hills", "Mt. Pinatubo",
"Boracay", "Big Ben", "North Pole"];
        placesToVisit.push("Boise");
        outputArray(placesToVisit);
        placesToVisit.splice(0, 2);
        document.write("</br>");
        outputArray();
        placesToVisit.sort();
        document.write("</br>");
        outputArray();

    </script>
</body>
</html>
```

CHAPTER 7 SUMMARY

In this chapter, we discussed working with arrays and how they can be accessed and manipulated.

We examined the basics of defining arrays, creating and declaring arrays and using for-loops to index arrays.

Also covered in this chapter are *push, pop, sort* and *splice*, which are methods for manipulating arrays.

In the next chapter we will be covering the string object.

CHAPTER 8
THE STRING OBJECT

CHAPTER OBJECTIVES:

- You will be able to understand what string object properties and methods are.
- You will learn how to alter string properties using methods.
- You will be able to replace strings with other strings via loops.
- You will learn how to count the number of characters a string has and return the result.
- You will also learn how to convert a comma separated string into an array.

8.1 OBJECT PROPERTIES AND METHODS

In this chapter we will concentrate on string objects. A great website reference for our discussion is:

www.w3schools.com/jsref/jsref_obj_string.asp

It is recommended that you open this webpage as you learn the lessons in this chapter.

We discussed strings earlier in the book and defined them as a series of letters and numbers. When working with strings we have generally surrounded the string itself with double quotes. String objects are no different—in fact, all strings are objects. This means, like all objects in Javascript, strings have properties that describe them and methods (a.k.a.: functions) that manipulate them.

When we say property, this is the attribute that is associated with the object that describes the object itself. In this lesson we will discuss the length property. Before moving on to that, let's briefly describe methods.

Methods are the actions or processes that can be applied or performed to the object. For a string object, examples would be changing from lowercase to uppercase, replacing with another string, removing a string and appending to the string.

When we create a string in Javascript we are creating a string object. You already know how to do this.

We'll assign a string to the variable *message.*

```
var message="Hello World!"
```

Next, we'll create another variable, here we'll use *x*, which will hold the length attribute of the variable *message:*

```
var x = message.length
```

In this example, *message* is the name of the string object and length is the property. If you display the value of *x*, you get the result 12.

var message="Hello World!"

Length Property Count: 1   2 3 4 5 6   7   8   9   10 11 12

Here is the complete code for displaying the length of the "Hello World!" string:

CODE LISTING: STRING PROPERTY--LENGTH

```
<!DOCTYPE html>
<html>
<head>
<title>Hello World!--Length</title>
</head>
<body>
    <script language="javascript"
type="text/javascript">
            var message = "Hello World!";
        var x=message.length;

    document.write("Length: " + x);
    document.write("</br>");
    </script>
```

```
</body>
</html>
```

This is the output of the above code displayed in Opera:

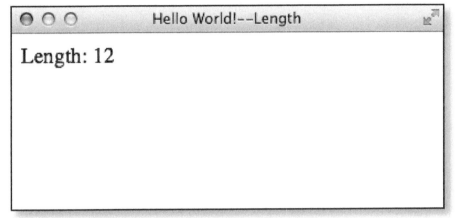

FIGURE 8 - 1

As another example, let's use the quote, "If you are strong enough, there are no precedents." from F. Scott Fitzgerald. Create a basic HTML document and include the script element in the body:

```
<script language="javascript" type="text/
javascript" >
```

Assign the quote to the variable *phrase* and close the script tag:

```
        var phrase = "If you are strong
enough, there are no precedents.";

</script>
```

Using length property, count the number of characters in the declared string. Display the quote using *document.write()* command, the correct syntax is:

```
document.write("length: " + phrase.length)
```

Following is the complete code listing:

```
<!DOCTYPE html>
<html>
<head>
<title>The String Object--Length</title>
</head>
<body>
    <script language="javascript"
type="text/javascript">
var phrase = "If you are strong enough,
there are no precedents.";

    document.write("Length: " + phrase.
length);
    document.write("</br>");
    </script>
</body>
</html>
```

The output of this code should look like:

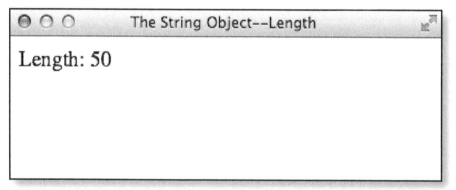

FIGURE 8 - 2

The spaces and special characters were included when the characters were counted, that is why the result is 50.

Now let's discuss some methods available with the string object. The first method we will talk about is **charAt()**. The *charAt()* method displays the character's position in the string. Like Javascript arrays, all strings are zero indexed.

charAt()

Using the same previous code listing, Display Object's Length, we will tweak the code so that *charAt()* is included.

We'll use a for-loop to iterate through the string one character at a time. Proper use of this function will ensure that every character position is scanned while going through the complete string set. The for-loop routine should look like:

```
for (var i=0; i < phrase.length; i++)
    {
        document.write(i + ": " + phrase.
charAt(i));
        document.write("</br>");
    }
```

The complete code routine for this exercise would be:

CODE LISTING: THE STRING OBJECT METHOD CHARAT()

```
<!DOCTYPE html>
<html>
<head>
<title>The String Method charAt()</title>
</head>
<body>
    <script language="javascript"
type="text/javascript">
var phrase = "If you are strong enough,
there are no precedents.";

    for (var i=0; i < phrase.length; i++)
    {
        document.write(i + ": " + phrase.
```

```
            charAt(i));
            document.write("</br>");
      }

      </script>
</body>
</html>
```

The output will look like this:

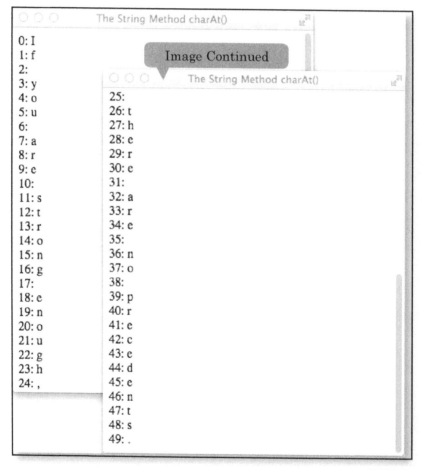

FIGURE 8 - 3

We used the for-loop technique to treat the string object like an array of characters.

The second method we are going to examine is **charCodeAt()**, which is used to display the Unicode value for a character at a particular index within a string. To demonstrate this, we simply append the following additional *document.write* command, containing the *charCodeAt()* function, right underneath the first *document.write* line in the for-loop routine:

charCodeAt()

```
document.write(" | " + phrase.
charCodeAt(i));
```

This method will display the Unicode value for each of the characters, including the space. Here is what the complete code should look like:

CODE LISTING: THE STRING OBJECT CHARCODEAT()

```
<!DOCTYPE html>
<html>
<head>
<title>The String Method charCodeAt()</
title>
</head>
<body>
<script language="javascript" type="text/
javascript">
var phrase = "If you are strong enough,
there are no precedents.";

    for (var i=0; i < phrase.length; i++)
    {
        document.write(i + ": " + phrase.
charAt(i));
                document.write(" | " +
phrase.charCodeAt(i));
        document.write("</br>");
    }
    </script>
</body>
</html>
```

Notice that the output displayed the letter at the string index first, followed by the pipe symbol (|) then by the corresponding Unicode of the character string:

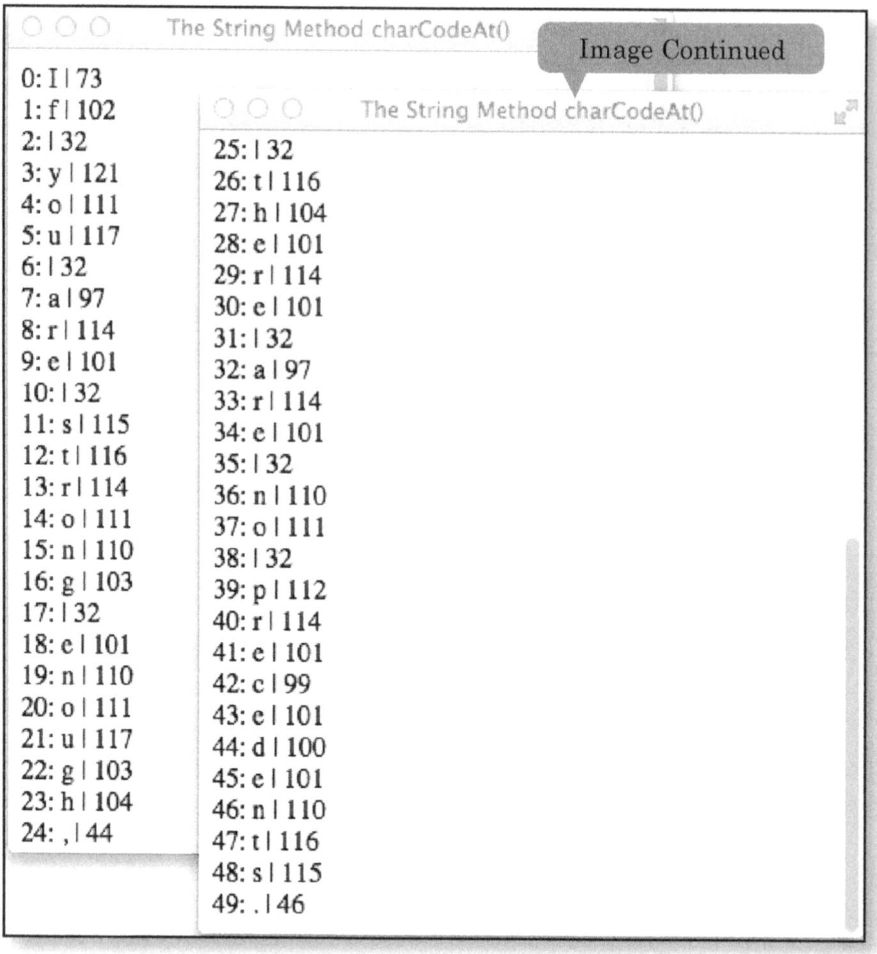

The String Method charCodeAt()

Image Continued

The String Method charCodeAt()

0: I | 73
1: f | 102
2: | 32
3: y | 121
4: o | 111
5: u | 117
6: | 32
7: a | 97
8: r | 114
9: e | 101
10: | 32
11: s | 115
12: t | 116
13: r | 114
14: o | 111
15: n | 110
16: g | 103
17: | 32
18: e | 101
19: n | 110
20: o | 111
21: u | 117
22: g | 103
23: h | 104
24: , | 44

25: | 32
26: t | 116
27: h | 104
28: e | 101
29: r | 114
30: e | 101
31: | 32
32: a | 97
33: r | 114
34: e | 101
35: | 32
36: n | 110
37: o | 111
38: | 32
39: p | 112
40: r | 114
41: e | 101
42: c | 99
43: e | 101
44: d | 100
45: e | 101
46: n | 110
47: t | 116
48: s | 115
49: . | 46

FIGURE 8 - 4

> *Unicode values can be used if one plans to alphabetize a series of string characters. Hint: lowercase characters have lower values than their uppercase counterparts.*

A third method that we're going to look at is **indexOf()**, which is used to find the first occurrence of a particular character within a string. For example, let's find out the index of the first lowercase "s" in the quote "If you are strong enough, there are no precedents."

indexOf()

Using *document.write*, the command line for the function would be:

```
document.write("Index of s: " + phrase.
indexOf('s'));
```

Write this command line just outside the function routine before the closing script tag. The complete code listing is:

CODE LISTING: THE STRING OBJECT INDEXOF()

```
<!DOCTYPE html>
<html>
<head>
<title>The String Method indexOf()</title>
</head>
<body>
    <script language="javascript"
type="text/javascript">
    var phrase = "If you are strong enough,
there are no precedents.";

    for  (var i=0; i < phrase.length; i++)
    {
        document.write(i + ": " + phrase.
charAt(i));
            document.write(" | " + phrase.
charCodeAt(i));
        document.write("</br>");
```

```
        }
                document.write("Index of s: "
+ phrase.indexOf('s'));
        </script>
</body>
</html>
```

The upper portion of the output would still look the same since we did not change the program code. However, you will notice that at the bottom portion, a new output line is displayed. This is the output of the *indexOf()* method. See the following images:

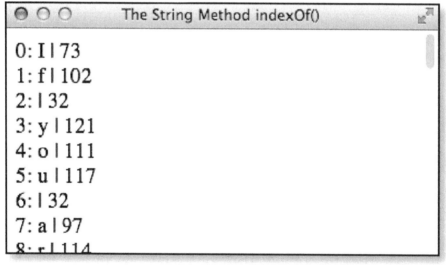

FIGURE 8 - 5

210   *Javascript for Beginners*

This image shows what you see when you scroll down further:

```
31:  | 32
32: a | 97
33: r | 114
34: e | 101
35:  | 32
36: n | 110
37: o | 111
38:  | 32
39: p | 112
40: r | 114
41: e | 101
42: c | 99
43: e | 101
44: d | 100
45: e | 101
46: n | 110
47: t | 116
48: s | 115
49: . | 46
Index of s: 11
```

indexOf() →

FIGURE 8 - 6

> *Notice that the result of the indexOf() command is shown at the bottom of the display window. The method returns a -1 if the specified text is not found.*

replace()

The fourth method we will introduce is **replace()**. This is used to replace a selected set of characters with a set of different characters, but does not alter the original string in the memory.

From the previous example, let's replace the word "strong" with "attractive". The command syntax for *replace()* when used in the example would be:

```
document.write(phrase.replace("strong",
"attractive"));
```

The complete code listing using *replace()* would be:

CODE LISTING: THE STRING OBJECT REPLACE()

```
<!DOCTYPE html>
<html>
<head>
<title>The String Method replace()</title>
</head>
<body>
   <script language="javascript"
type="text/javascript">
   var phrase = "'If you are strong enough,
there are no precedents.'";
document.write(phrase);
document.write("</br></br>");
document.write("After using the replace()
method:</br></br>");
                   document.write(phrase.
replace("strong","attractive"));
   document.write("</br></br>");
       document.write("Invoking the
command document.write(phrase) without
another replace() instruction, the result
is: </br></br>");

      document.write(phrase);
   </script>
</body>
</html>
```

The output might look like this:

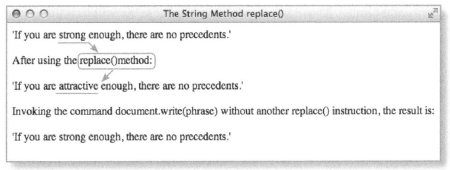

FIGURE 8 - 7

Notice how the content of the variable *phrase* was left unchanged, even if the method *replace()* has been introduced. It did not change the variable's content in the memory, but instead merely affected the displayed value superficially.

This time, let's create a string variable called *names* whose value is a series of names separated by commas:

```
var names = "Jack, Jill, John, Jane,
Johnny";
```

This is just a string with commas in it.

Using this string set, let us introduce and demonstrate the last method we're going to look at called **split()**, which we will use to convert the string contained by *names* into an array.

split()

To *split* the string, another variable must be introduced to hold the resulting array. Let us use *moreNames* to catch the returned array after implementing the *split()* method on the original string variable *names*. This is how the code should appear:

```
var names = "Jack, Jill, John, Jane,
Johnny"; var moreNames = names.split(",");
```

Notice that within the split method's parentheses we placed a comma. This argument indicates to the split method what character we want to use as a delimiter. The elements of the resulting array will be split on the delimiting character.

Next, we'll introduce a for-loop to iterate through the new *moreNames* array. The code for the for-loop:

```
for(var x=0; x < moreNames.length; x++)
{
    document.write(moreNames[x]);
    document.write("<br/>");
}
```

Here's the complete code listing demonstrating the split method of the string object:

CODE LISTING: THE STRING METHOD SPLIT()

```
<!DOCTYPE html>
<html>
<head>
<title>The String Method split()</title>
</head>
<body>
    <script language="javascript"
type="text/javascript">

    var names = "Jack, Jill, John, Jane,
Johnny";
        document.write(names);
document.write("<br/>After using the
split() method, here is the result:<br/>");
        var moreNames = names.split(',');
    document.write("<br/>");

        for(var x = 0; x < moreNames.
length; x++)
```

```
      {
              document.write(moreNames[x]);
              document.write("</br>");
      }
    </script>
  </body>
  </html>
```

This is the how the output should appear in the browser:

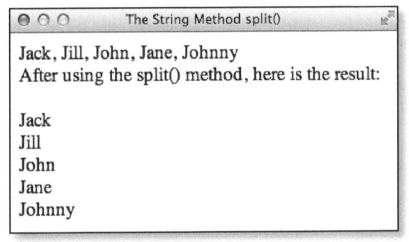

Jack, Jill, John, Jane, Johnny
After using the split() method, here is the result:

Jack
Jill
John
Jane
Johnny

FIGURE 8 - 8

We have just demonstrated how an array can be extracted from a string value that is separated by commas using the *split()* method.

CHAPTER 8 LAB EXERCISE

1) Create a new HTML document.

2) Insert Javascript tags. Inside them, declare a variable called *poem*.

3) Add the following text to *poem*. Use the <br/> tag at the end of each line to create line breaks.

With Rue My Heart is Laden
by Alfred Edward Housman, 1896

With rue my heart is laden
For golden friends I had,
For many a rose-lipt maiden
And many a lightfoot lad.

By brooks too broad for leaping
The lightfoot boys are laid;
The rose-lipt girls are sleeping
In fields where roses fade.

4) Create a loop to iterate through the string one letter at a time. Create a new string variable and within the loop, access each character in the poem from the first character to the final character.

5) While in the loop, if the character is a vowel, replace it with an X and add that character to the new string. If the letter is a consonant, simply add it to the new string. The output should look like this:

WXth RXX My HXXrt Xs LXdXn
by AlfrXd EdwXrd HXXsmXn, 1896

WXth rXX my hXXrt Xs lXdXn
FXr gXldXn frXXnds I hXd,
FXr mXny X rXsX-lXpt mXXdXn
And mXny X lXghtfXXt lXd.

By brXXks tXX brXXd fXr lXXpXng
ThX lXghtfXXt bXys XrX lXXd;
ThX rXsX-lXpt gXrls XrX slXXpXng
In fXXlds whXrX rXsXs fXdX.

> Notice that uppercase vowels and the 'y' in 'my' and 'by' were left out in this solution. Don't worry about them yet, we'll explain those later.

6) Create a new variable and assign it the value: "tennis, ice hockey, baseball, basketball, football, soccer, bowling".

7) Using the appropriate string manipulation method, convert it into an array with each sport assigned an array index.

8) Sort the array alphabetically, then display the output.

CHAPTER 8 LAB SOLUTION

```
<!DOCTYPE html>
<html>
<head>
<title>Lab Exercise 8</title>
</head>
<body>
    <script language="javascript"
type="text/javascript">

    var poem = " With Rue My Heart is Laden
</br>"
            + " by Alfred Edward Housman,
1896 </br></br>"
            + "With rue my heart is laden"
+ "</br>"
            + "For golden friends I had,"
+ "</br>"
            + "For many a rose-lipt
maiden" + "</br>"
            + "And many a lightfoot lad."
+ "</br></br>"
            + "By brooks too broad for
leaping" + "</br>"
            + "The lightfoot boys are
laid;" + "</br>"
            + "The rose-lipt girls are
sleeping" + "</br>"
            + "In fields where roses
fade.";

    for (var y=0; y<poem.length; y++)
    {
        var vowels = /[aeiou]/g;
        var poemReplaced = poem.
```

```javascript
    replace(vowels, 'X');
    }
    document.write(poemReplaced);

    var sports = "tennis, ice hockey,
baseball, basketball, football, soccer,
bowling";
    var sportsS = sports.split(',');
    document.write("</br>")
    document.write("</br>")

    for (var z = 0; z<sportsS.length; z++)
    {
        sportsS.sort();
        document.write(sportsS[z] + "</
br>");
    }

    </script>
</body>
</html>
```

This is how the output should appear:

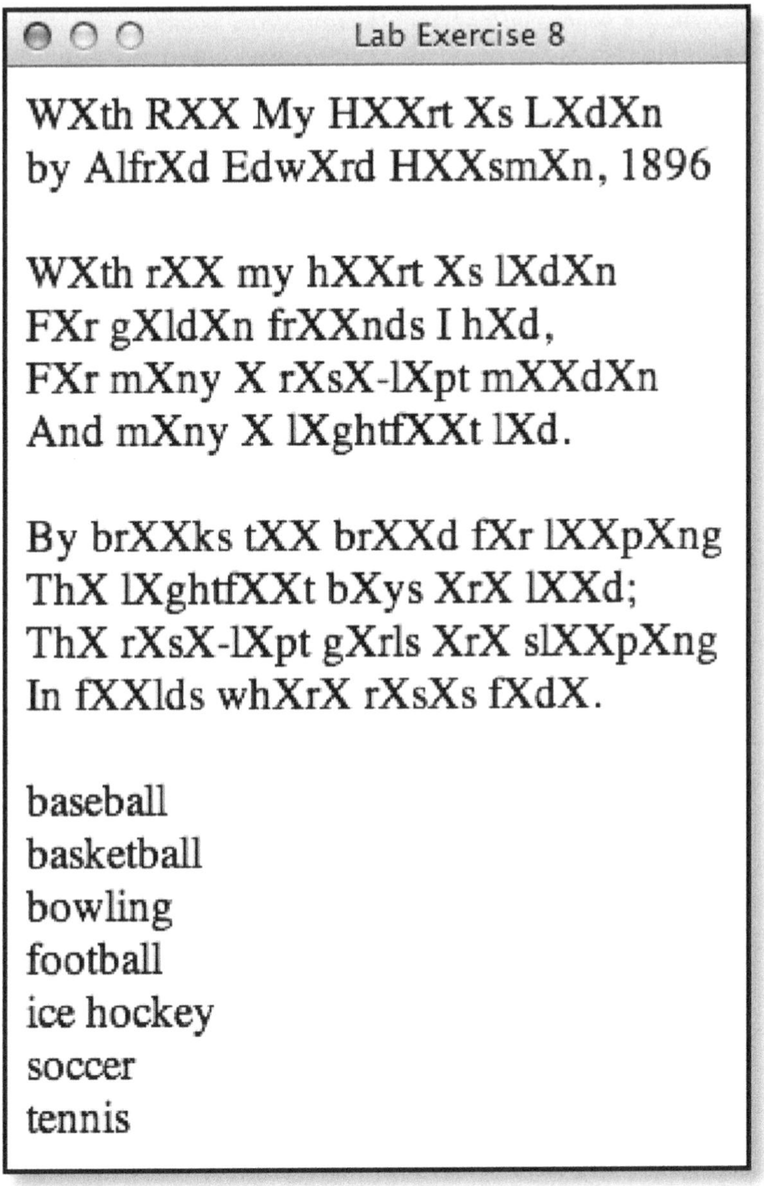

```
●  ○  ○                Lab Exercise 8

WXth RXX My HXXrt Xs LXdXn
by AlfrXd EdwXrd HXXsmXn, 1896

WXth rXX my hXXrt Xs lXdXn
FXr gXldXn frXXnds I hXd,
FXr mXny X rXsX-lXpt mXXdXn
And mXny X lXghtfXXt lXd.

By brXXks tXX brXXd fXr lXXpXng
ThX lXghtfXXt bXys XrX lXXd;
ThX rXsX-lXpt gXrls XrX slXXpXng
In fXXlds whXrX rXsXs fXdX.

baseball
basketball
bowling
football
ice hockey
soccer
tennis
```

FIGURE 8 - 9

Final Lab Solutions 219

Notice in the poem's output how the uppercase vowels and the letter y—grammatically used here as a vowel—were not replaced with 'X'. This is because Javascript is case sensitive—it doesn't recognize 'a' as being the same as 'A'. As programmers, it is our task to make sure we include the remaining uppercase vowel characters in the variable assignment so they will also be replaced with 'X'.

The case for 'y' is not as simple. The algorithm to determine which words use 'y' as a vowel has to be taken into account. Hint: Add a conditional routine that will determine what words have the letter 'y' used as a vowel in them, and will have to be added in the complete code listing. Figuring out how to replace the 'y' characters will be left as an activity challenge for you.

Modify the program now so it includes the uppercase vowels in the *replace()* exercise. Here is what the revised line should look like:

```
var vowels = /[aeiouAEIOU]/g;
```

CHAPTER 8 SUMMARY

In this chapter, we discussed the string property *length* which is used to count the number of characters contained by a string.

We also discussed five string manipulation methods:

charAt()	which is used to display the specific location of a character in the set of strings
charCodeAt()	which returns the Unicode value of a string character
indexOf()	which is used to find out where something occurs in the string
replace()	which is used to replace a selected set of strings with different string values
split()	which is used to convert strings separated by commas into an array

TABLE 8 - 1

We also showed how string characters can be manipulated using iterations and how certain string sets can be replaced with another character and display the results or changes.

In the next chapter, we will be discussing how to obtain and manipulate user's browser window information.

Javascript for Beginners

CHAPTER 9

OBTAINING AND MANIPULATING USER INFORMATION

CHAPTER OBJECTIVES:

• You will learn how to obtain user's browser window information and manipulate this information.
• You will be able to use the navigator object.
• You will learn how to use the windows object.
• You will be able to manipulate information using screen object.

9.1 NAVIGATOR OBJECT

In this chapter, you will learn how to use Javascript to obtain information about the user's browser such as code, name, and version. You will also learn about the window properties, *inner width* and *inner height*. We will also talk about the screen information—*height* and *color depth*, and how to manipulate all these Javascript objects using methods.

Oftentimes when developing web applications it is useful to gather information about the user's environment. This information is often used to optimize the user's experience or execute processes specific to the user's environment. Javascript has a rich set of objects and methods to help us do that.

The first object we will discuss is the navigator object. The keyword used to work with this object is **navigator** (surprise!). Along with this object, we can employ the following properties:

> **appCodename**, which is used to disclose the browser's codename, (for example, Mozilla)

> **appName**, which identifies the name of the browser used, for example, Netscape

> **appVersion,** which reports the current version of the browser used

This is the code listing that uses navigator object and properties to obtain and display some basic browser information.

CODE LISTING: NAVIGATOR OBJECT

```
<!DOCTYPE html>

<html>
<head>
    <title>Navigator Object</title>
</head>
    <script language="javascript"
type="text/javascript">
        document.write("Code name of the
Browser: " + navigator.appCodename);
        document.write("</br>Name of
Browser: " + navigator.appName);
        document.write("</br>Version of
Browser: " + navigator.appVersion);
    </script>
<body>
</body>
</html>
```

This is an example of how the output will look when viewed in Opera:

appCodename
appName
appVersion

FIGURE 9 - 1

When viewed in Internet Explorer:

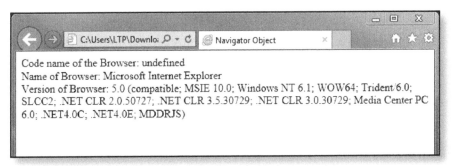

FIGURE 9 - 2

When viewed in Chrome:

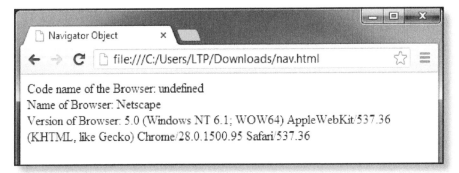

FIGURE 9 - 3

When viewed in Firefox:

FIGURE 9 - 4

Note that these results may be different from yours when you run the same code on your computer.

9.2 WINDOW OBJECTS

Now we'll examine the window object. The properties under the window object are: **document**, which specifies the document type but does not return a value; **innerWidth**, which tells the browser window's inner width in pixels; **innerHeight**, which tells the inner height of the browser window in pixels; **location**, which tells the URL where the current webpage or document page is stored or located; and **protocol**, a property of "location", which indicates the web page protocol used, whether it's http or https.

Both *dimension* and *location* objects return a value when called or implemented.

The first window object we will demonstrate is *document*. The command syntax for the *document* object would be:

```
document.write(window.document);
```

Some strings may be concatenated for use with the *window.document*. For example:

```
document.write("Document: " + window.
document);
```

Integrating the code in the complete code listing, it should look like this:

CODE LISTING: WINDOW OBJECT -- DOCUMENT

```
<!DOCTYPE html>

<html>
<head>
    <title>Window Object--Document</title>
</head>

<body>
    <script language="javascript"
type="text/javascript">
```

```
        document.write("Document: " +
window.document);
    </script>
</body>
</html>
```

This is how the output will look when viewed in different browsers:

When viewed in Opera:

FIGURE 9 - 5

When viewed in Internet Explorer:

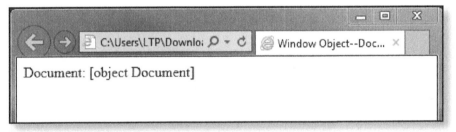

FIGURE 9 - 6

When viewed in Chrome:

FIGURE 9 - 7

When viewed in Firefox:

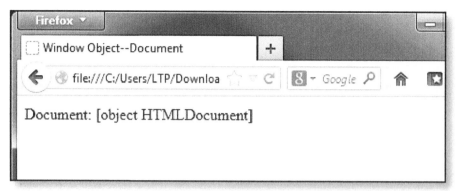

FIGURE 9 - 8

The second and third window object properties we will demonstrate are the *innerWidth* and *innerHeight*. The command syntax for these objects is:

```
document.write("Width: " + window.
innerWidth);
document.write("Height: " + window.
innerHeight);
```

Integrating the code into a complete code listing, we have:

CODE LISTING: WINDOW OBJECT – DIMENSION

```
<!DOCTYPE html>

<html>
<head>
    <title>Window Object--Dimension</title>
</head>

<body>
    <script language="javascript"
type="text/javascript">
        document.write("Width: " + window.
innerWidth);
```

```
        document.write("<br/>");
        document.write("Height: " + window.
innerHeight);
    </script>
</body>
</html>
```

This is how the output will appear in the browser:

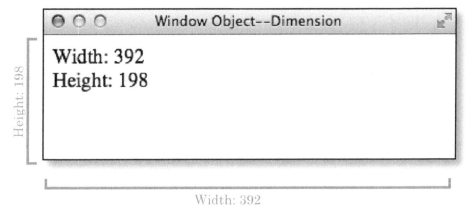

Drag the corner of the window to resize it, then click refresh. Notice how it returns a different value.

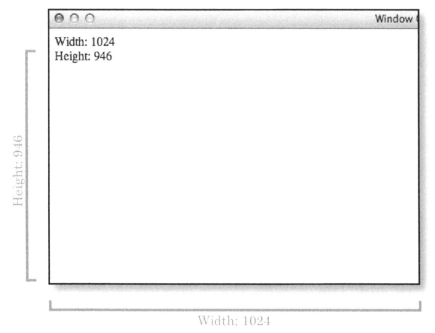

FIGURE 9 - 10

We can also set the *inner width* and *inner height* of the browser.

The command syntax is:

```
window.innerWidth=value in pixels;
window.innerHeight=value in pixels;
```

Using these in the complete code listing, we'll have:

CODE LISTING: INNERWIDTH AND INNERHEIGHT

```
<!DOCTYPE html>

<html>
<head>
    <title>Window Object--Setting Width and
Height</title>
```

```
</head>
<body>
    <script language="javascript"
type="text/javascript">
window.innerWidth=300;
window.innerHeight=200;
        document.write("Width: " + window.
innerWidth);
document.write("<br/>");
        document.write("Height: " + window.
innerHeight);
    </script>
</body>
</html>
```

Here is the output when viewed in the browser:

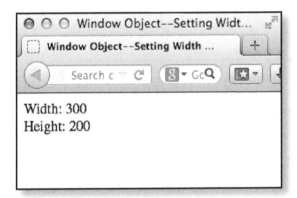

FIGURE 9 - 11

Care must be observed when using dimension properties (*innerWidth* and *innerHeight*) as they exhibit varied reactions and implement differently in different browsers. There are instances that browsers do not respond accordingly with these inner window settings.

The third object we will discuss is *location*. This object can do one of two things: get the current page address or URL, or redirect the browser to a new page location. The command syntax for getting the location object is:

```
document.write(window.location);
```

Integrating the code in a complete code listing:

CODE LISTING: WINDOW OBJECT -- GETTING THE LOCATION

```
<!DOCTYPE html>
<html>
<head>
    <title>Window Object--Location</title>
</head>

<body>
    <script language="javascript"
type="text/javascript">
        document.write("Location: " +
window.location);
    </script>
</body>
</html>
```

Here is what the output will look like when viewed in a browser window:

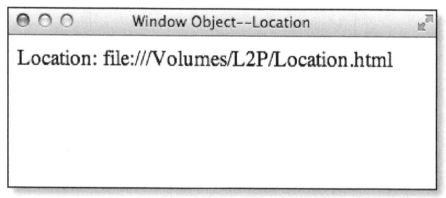

FIGURE 9 - 12

Now let's discuss how to set the *location object*.
The command syntax for setting the *location object* would be:

```
window.location = "page URL";
```

For example:

```
window.location = "http://www.cnn.com";
```

Integrating the code in a complete code listing:

CODE LISTING: WINDOW OBJECT – SETTING THE LOCATION

```
<!DOCTYPE html>
<html>
<head>
    <title>Window Object--Setting the
Location</title>
</head>

<body>
    <script language="javascript"
type="text/javascript">
        window.location="http://www.cnn.
com";
    </script>
</body>
</html>
```

Following is the output when viewed in the browser:

FIGURE 9 - 13

A property that can be used along with the location object is **protocol**. See the following code listing where the *location* referred to is a file:

CODE LISTING: WINDOW OBJECT – LOCATION PROTOCOL

```
<!DOCTYPE html>

<html>
<head>
    <title>Window Object--Location
Protocol</title>
</head>
```

```
<body>
    <script language="javascript"
type="text/javascript">
        document.write("Location protocol:
" + window.location.protocol);
    </script>
</body>
</html>
```

Following is the output when viewed in the browser:

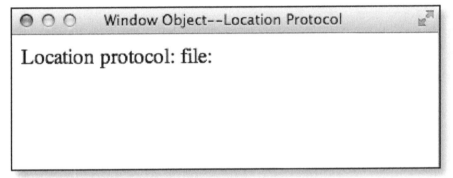

Location protocol: file:

FIGURE 9 - 14

Notice in this example that the returned value is "file:" because the source page being viewed is from a local file. If it was a browser being viewed, it would return either "http:" or "https:".

Let's see how the returned value changes when a *location object* is changed to a web page.

CODE LISTING: WEB LOCATION PROTOCOL

```
<!DOCTYPE html>
<html>
<head>
</head>
```

```
<body>
    <script>
        document.write("Location protocol:
" + window.location.protocol);
    </script>
</body>
</html>
```

In the event that the browser you are using does not display the output as expected, try running the code in the www.w3school.com "Tryit Editor v 1.6 window", and the output will be displayed as:

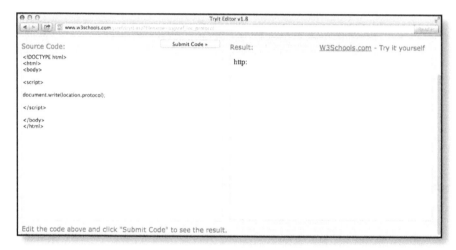

FIGURE 9 - 15

9.3 SCREEN OBJECT

Let's look at the **screen object,** which returns information about the actual monitor screen being used. Using the screen object, we can determine the screen *height* in pixels and *color depth* of the user's display unit.

The command syntax for implementing the screen object *height* and *color depth* is:

```
document.write("Screen Height: " + screen.
height);
document.write("Color Depth: " + screen.
colorDepth);
```

Integrating the code in the complete code listing, we have:

CODE LISTING: SCREEN OBJECT

```
<!DOCTYPE html>
<html>
<head>
    <title> Screen Object</title>
</head>

<body>
    <script language="javascript"
type="text/javascript">
        document.write("Screen Height: " +
screen.height);
        document.write("<br/>");
        document.write("Screen Color Depth:
" + screen.colorDepth);
    </script>
</body>
</html>
```

This is how the output will look:

FIGURE 9 - 16

The *screen height* value that was returned came from the monitor's height setting on the same computer where the above code was run. See the following image:

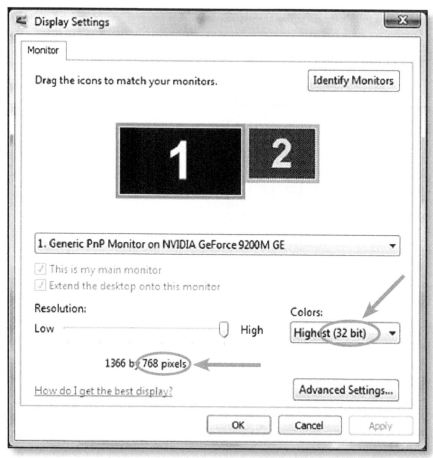

FIGURE 9 - 17

The color depth value came from the monitor's display settings. It can be verified that it refers to the color setting of the monitor. Refer to the following image:

FIGURE 9 - 18

As you can see, information such as window settings and user screen information can be obtained through properties and methods in Javascript.

This is very helpful when trying to identify the browser window and screen attributes of a user's window environment. It helps us adjust the window display setting accordingly so that an application can give the user the best possible experience.

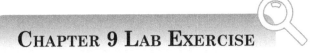

CHAPTER 9 LAB EXERCISE

1) Create a new HTML5 document. Include the Javascript tags.

2) Using the *navigator object* and *document.write()*, display the browser name, browser version, and if cookies are enabled or not.

3) Using the screen object properties and *document.write()*, display the height and width of the screen.

4) Examine the documentation for the *window object* located at http://www.w3schools.com/jsref/obj_window.asp. Identify and select the appropriate method(s) and move the window to the top left-hand corner of the screen. Change the window size to 300 pixels by 300 pixels.

5) Run your Chapter Lab Exercise Solution in at least three different browsers. Take note of any differences.

```
<!DOCTYPE html>

<html>
<head>
<title>Chapter 9 Lab Solution</title>
<head>
    <title>Chapter 9 Lab Solution</title>
</head>
<body>
    <script language="javascript"
type="text/javascript">
        document.write("Browser Name: " +
navigator.appName);
        document.write("<br/>Browser
Version: " + navigator.appVersion);
        document.write("<br/>Cookies: " +
navigator.cookieEnabled);
        document.write("<br/>Screen Width:
" + screen.width);
        document.write("<br/>Screen Height:
" + screen.height);

        window.moveTo(0,0);
        window.resizeTo(300,300);
        document.write("<br/>Window Inner
Width: " + window.innerWidth);
        document.write("<br/>Window Inner
Height: " + window.innerHeight);
    </script>
</body>
</html>
```

This is how the output will appear in a web browser:

Browser Name: Netscape
Browser Version: 5.0 (Windows)
Cookies: true
Screen Width: 1366
Screen Height: 768
Window Inner Width: 300
Window Inner Height: 300

FIGURE 9 - 19

Most browsers claim they already support *moveTo* and the *innerHeight* and *innerWidth* properties, but in actuality, they are still having some errors displaying/implementing them. As of this writing, only Firefox had consistent results compared to other browsers.

CHAPTER 9 SUMMARY

In this chapter, we discussed obtaining and manipulating a user's browser and screen information.

We talked about the following navigator objects:

appCodename	which is used to disclose the browser's codename
appName	which identifies the name of the browser used
appVersion	which reports the current version of the browser used

TABLE 9 - 1

We discussed window objects which are used to manipulate the browser's inner width and inner height.

Also discussed was the *window location object* which is used to obtain the current page address/URL or to redirect the browser to a new page. Another window location property presented is *protocol*. This property tells the protocol used—file, http or https.

We also covered the *screen object*, which is used to obtain the *screen height* of the actual monitor in pixel units and the *color depth* or resolution in bits.

In the next and final chapter we will talk about the *document object*.

CHAPTER 10

DOCUMENT OBJECT AND innerHTML PROPERTIES

CHAPTER OBJECTIVES:
- You will be able to extract text from text boxes and display extracted text using alert box.
- You will learn how to highlight texts using color background.
- You will be able to change page content within a page without popping out a new window.
- You will learn how to install Firebug and how it is used to see the changes in codes taking place in a page.

10.1 DOCUMENT OBJECT

In this final chapter (whew!), we will present the overview of the document object and *innerHTML* properties. We will also introduce a Firefox utility called Firebug, which enables you to view changes in code as the page content changes.

Let's first discuss document object. When we say **document object**, we're referring to both internal browser settings and the elements that are found or placed within an HTML page document. The document object is stored in the browser in a hierarchical format and effectively serves as memory or RAM for your Javascript programs. The entire state of the browser is stored in the document object—including your HTML, Javascript, and CSS code. There are standardized ways of working with the document object and its various properties (hundreds of them). This standardized model—which is fairly consistent across browsers—is known as the **document object model**.

Some examples of document objects: text fields, reply buttons, hyperlinks, etc.

The **innerHTML property** provides a way to access different facets of the document object—specifically those that are designed to hold HTML code. The innerHTML property allows you both to retrieve and set the

HTML in a document object node.

By taking advantage of the document object model, you can adjust almost anything within the browser—including the CSS that is styling your content. It is important to understand that what is stored in the document object is dynamic, so the values may change as the user interacts with the website. For example, if the user types information into a form, the information is stored in the document object where you may access it—before it is submitted to the server.

First, let us create a HTML document that will have three elements in it: two text input fields and a button. These elements will be manipulated using the innerHTML property and document object.

In our HTML document body, include the elements *first* and *last* as text boxes and a button labeled with the text "Press Me". The button will trigger a function called *processName()* via the onclick event. This is how the body element will be coded:

```
<body>
    First: <input type= "text" id= "first"/>
    <br/>
    Last: <input type= "text" id= "last"/>
<input type= "button" value= "Press Me"
onclick= "processName()"/>
</body>
```

The function *processName()* will extract the values input in the *first* and *last* text box elements. Before we get to that, make sure that you write the script tag in the head element of the HTML document like so:

```
<script language="javascript" type="text/
javascript">
```

Then let's declare two local variables—*first* and *last*—which will be used to hold or contain the values that will be extracted from the text box elements.

```
var first;
var last;
```

Now initialize these variables by assigning the method **getElementById().value**, to extract the values from the text boxes. The code should look like this:

```
first=document.getElementById('first').value;
last=document.getElementById('last').value;
```

Be sure to include *.value* because without it, only the text box will be extracted—not the values inside the text box elements.

Here's all the code we've written so far:

```
<script language="javascript" type="text/
javascript">
    function processName()
    {
            var first;
            var last;
            first=document.getElementById.(
'first').value;
            last=document.getElementById.(
'last').value;
```

To make it easy, we'll use an alert box to display the extracted values. Here is the alert code:

```
alert(first + " " + last);
```

The complete code listing:

CODE LISTING: THE DOCUMENT OBJECT WITH ALERT BOX

```html
<!DOCTYPE html>
<html>
<head>
    <title>The Document Object </title>
    <script language="javascript"
type="text/javascript">
    function processName()
    {
        var first;
        var last;
        first = document.
getElementById('first').value;
        last = document.
getElementById('last').value;

        alert(first + " " + last);
    }
    </script>
</head>

<body>
    Please type in your first and last name:
    <br/><br/>
    First: <input type="text" id="first" />
    <br/>
    Last: <input type="text" id="last" />
    <input type="button" value="Press Me!"
onclick="processName()"/>
</body>
</html>
```

The execution of the program in the browser should appear as follows:

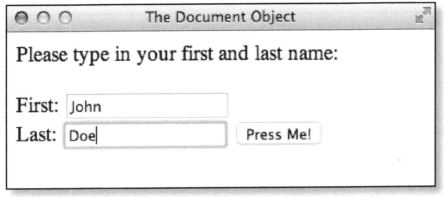

FIGURE 10 - 1

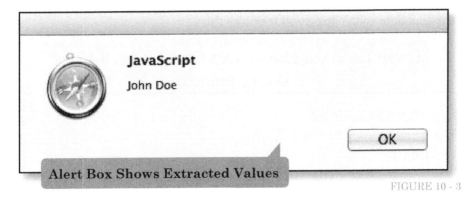

FIGURE 10 - 2

FIGURE 10 - 3

Let us add another *document object—a paragraph <p></p>*.

Add the paragraph tags to the body of the document with the content: "This is John's paragraph. The quick brown fox jumps over the lazy dog."

The *paragraph* tag should look like this:

```
<p>This is John's paragraph. The quick
brown fox jumps over the lazy dog.</p>
```

To make the paragraph retrieveable through the document object, we must add an id attribute and value to the paragraph element. We're going to use "para" as the value. This will allow us to use the method **document.getElementById()** to retrieve the paragraph element and manipulate it in Javascript.

```
<p id="para">This is John's paragraph. The
quick brown fox jumps over the lazy dog.
</p>
```

Using the *document object*, let's apply some CSS styling in the paragraph by adding the following to the script:

```
document.getElementById("para").style.
backgroundColor="99FFFF";
```

The complete code listing will look like this:

CODE LISTING: DOCUMENT OBJECT WITH FONT BACKGROUND

```
<!DOCTYPE html>
<html>
<head>
    <title>The Document Object</title>
    <script language="javascript"
type="text/javascript">
    function processName()
```

```
    {
        var first;
        var last;
        first = document.
getElementById("first").value;
        last = document.
getElementById("last").value;

        alert(first + " " + last);

        document.getElementById("para").
style.backgroundColor = "#99FFFF";     //
sets the highlight color to aqua blue
    }
    </script>
</head>

<body>
    Please type in your first and last name:
    <br/><br/>
    First: <input type="text" id="first" />
    <br/>
    Last: <input type="text" id="last" />
    <input type="button" value="Press Me!"
onclick="processName()"/>

    <p id="para"> This is John's paragraph.
The quick brown fox jumps over the lazy
dog.</p>
</body>
</html>
```

This code will turn the background color of the *paragraph* aqua blue after applying the style. This is how the output should appear:

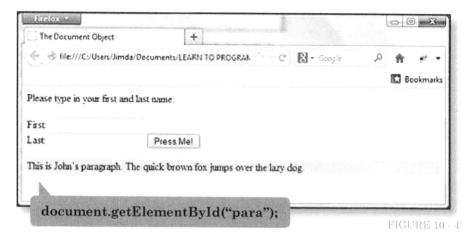

FIGURE 10 - 4

Another style that can be applied through the document object is bold font. To accomplish this, we'll add another *document.getElementById* command but replace the CSS attribute "background" with "fontWeight" and assign the value "bold". This is how the command line should look:

```
document.getElementById('para').style.
fontWeight="bold";
```

The complete code listing should look like this:

Code Listing: The Document Object with Bold Font Background

```
<!DOCTYPE html>
<html>
<head>
    <title>The Document Object</title>
    <script language="javascript"
type="text/javascript">
    function processName()
    {
        var first;
```

```
        var last;
        first = document.
getElementById('first').value;
        last = document.
getElementById('last').value;

        alert(first + " " + last);
                document.
getElementById('para').style.
backgroundColor = "#99ffff"; // sets the
background color aqua blue behind the text
        document.getElementById('para').
style.fontWeight = "bold";
    }
    </script>
</head>

<body>
    Please type in your first and last name:
    <br/><br/>
    First: <input type="text" id="first" />
    <br/>
    Last: <input type="text" id="last" />
    <input type="button" value="Press Me!"
onclick="processName()"/>

    <p id="para"> This is John's paragraph.
The quick brown fox jumps over the lazy
dog.</p>
</body>
</html>
```

This is how the output should look:

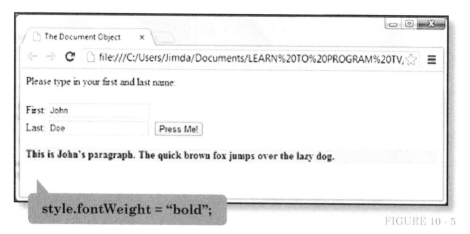

FIGURE 10 - 5

Changing the look and feel of document objects and elements using CSS is a powerful ability. It enhances a web page developer's capability to effectively deliver sequences of events or changes in the webpage without needing to modify the codes from the server side, thus creating dynamic styling in Javascript.

If you're familiar with CSS, you've probably noted that the CSS syntax is generally respected when modified through the document object and the style property. Any CSS rule that you can create in a style sheet can be created dynamically with the document object and style property.

10.2 THE INNERHTML PROPERTY

The **innerHTML** property is used to access the HTML inside any element within the HTML code. For example, a <p> paragraph element may have text and other HTML tags inside it. By using the innerHTML property, we can access the content to both retrieve and modify it.

http://javascript.about.com/library/bldom06.htm uses this explanation of what innerHTML is:

> *The most useful property of our web page objects... The innerHTML property was introduced by Microsoft in Internet Explorer as a convenient way of being able to access the entire content of the HTML container all at once. It turned out to be so convenient that all of the other browsers quickly added support for this property.*

We can use innerHTML either to retrieve the current content of the container or to insert new content into that container.

Let's dig in and start modifying content in an HTML document through Javascript. First, we create a basic HTML document, then add a logical division. Then, place script tags in the head of the document:

```
<!DOCTYPE html>
<html>
<head>
<title>
</title>
    <script language="javascript"
type="text/javascript">

    </script>
</head>
```

Now, we'll make the div accessible through the document object and Javascript by adding an id attribute and value. We'll make the value "content":

```
<body>
    <div id="content">
```

Next, let's add a paragraph element. Of course, it must be enclosed by the paragraph tags. Then we'll close the "div":

```
    <p>This paragraph will change when the
document object's innerHTML property is
accessed.</p>
    </div>
```

To make it a little more interesting, let's add a button that, when clicked, will call a function that will contain the code that will dynamically alter the HTML. The segment code for the button is as follows:

```
<input type="button " value="Press Me! "
onclick="changeContent()"/>
</body>
</html>
```

Let's go back to the head of the document—right between the script tags—and insert the function *changeContent()* inside the tags, thereby forming an element.

This is how the inserted code should look:

```
function changeContent()
    {
    document.getElementById('content').
innerHTML = "<h3>See? The content has
changed!</h3>";
    }
```

We used <h3> header 3 for the content so that the change will be pretty obvious once it occurs. The complete code listing should now look like:

CODE LISTING: INNERHTML CHANGE "DIV" CONTENT

```
<!DOCTYPE html>
<html>
<head>
<title>Inner HTML - Change "div" Content</
title>
   <script language="javascript"
type="text/javascript">
   function changeContent()
   {
           document.
getElementById('content').innerHTML =
"<h3>See? the content has changed!</h3>";
   }
   </script>
</head>
<body>
   <div id="content">
   <p>This paragraph will change when
the document object's innerHTML property
is accessed, that is, when you press the
button.</p>
   </div>
   <input type="button" value="Press Me!"
onclick="changeContent()"/>
</body>
</html>
```

The output should look like this:

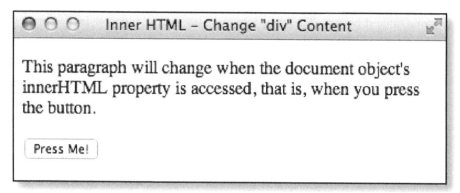

FIGURE 10 - 6

After clicking on the button:

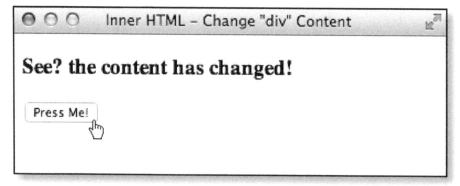

FIGURE 10 - 7

We can get an insiders view to what's happening in the browser with a plug in called Firebug. Firebug can show you what is actually happening within the document object as the button is pressed.

First you have to download Firebug and add it to the Firefox browser. The add-on may be downloaded from this site:
https://addons.mozilla.org/en-US/firefox/addon/firebug/

After downloading, you will see a prompt like this:

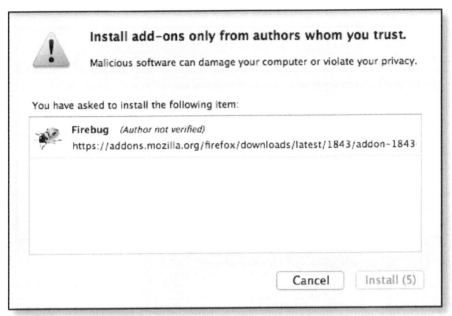

FIGURE 10 - 8

The following images depict how to trace what is happening within our program using Firebug.

Notice the little image in the upper right corner of the Firefox browser that looks like a bug (inside the circle). This confirms that the Firefox add-on tool, Firebug, is installed in the browser.

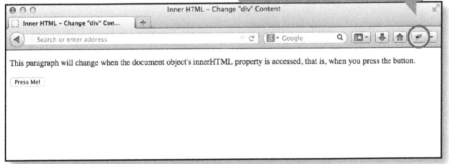

FIGURE 10 - 9

Click the little image of the bug and this is what you will see in your browser:

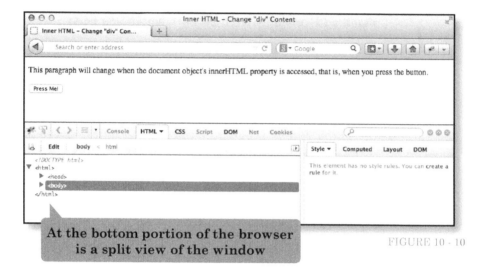

FIGURE 10 - 10

When you hover your mouse over the <body> line of the elements list, this is what gets displayed at the upper portion of the window:

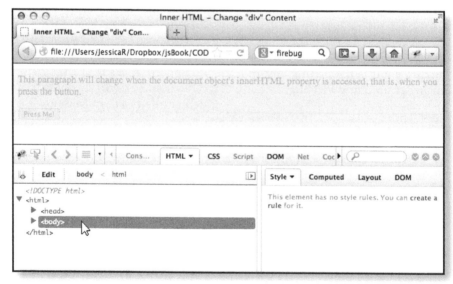

FIGURE 10 - 11

I'll stretch the window so it can accommodate the rest of the code as I expand the head and body of the HTML document.

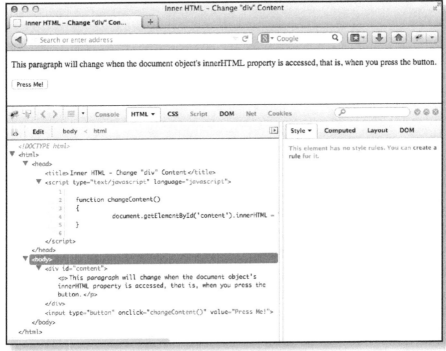

FIGURE 10 - 12

The window now displays the entire code of our Change 'div' Content Program Routine.

Hover the mouse over any of the HTML element code lines and you will either see a plain blue highlight:

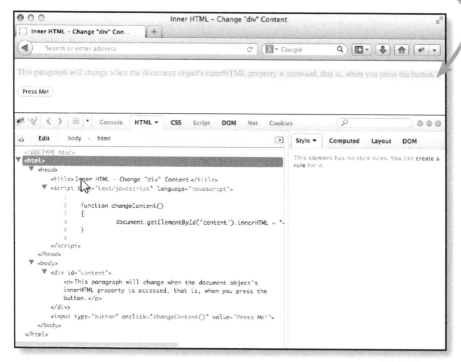

FIGURE 10 - 13

260   *Javascript for Beginners*

Or you will see a blue box highlighted by yellow (here it shows the entire paragraph element) in the upper portion of the window:

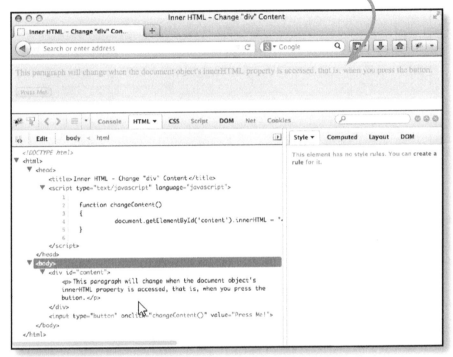

FIGURE 10 - 14

The reason we really want to explore Firebug is to see what happens when the event is triggered and what happens to the HTML code via the innerHTML property.

Let's get another close look at the code before the "Press Me" button is clicked:

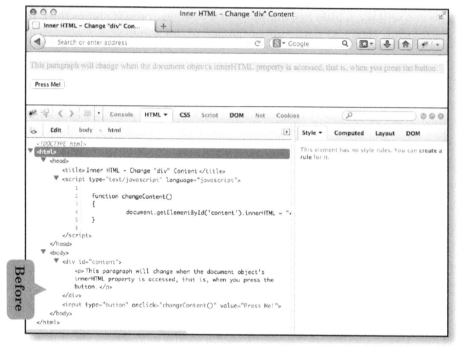

FIGURE 10 - 15

Now click the "Press Me" button. This is what we immediately see after the button is clicked:

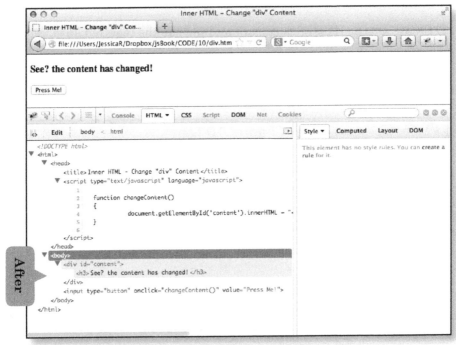

FIGURE 10 - 16

Compare the paragraph elements of both screenshot images and see how the latter has changed. You get the same result when you view the code listing using Firebug in your browser.

Chapter 10 Lab Exercise

1) Create a basic HTML5 document and include the required Javascript tags.

2) Populate the document with five HTML elements: four textbox fields and a Submit button. See the following image:

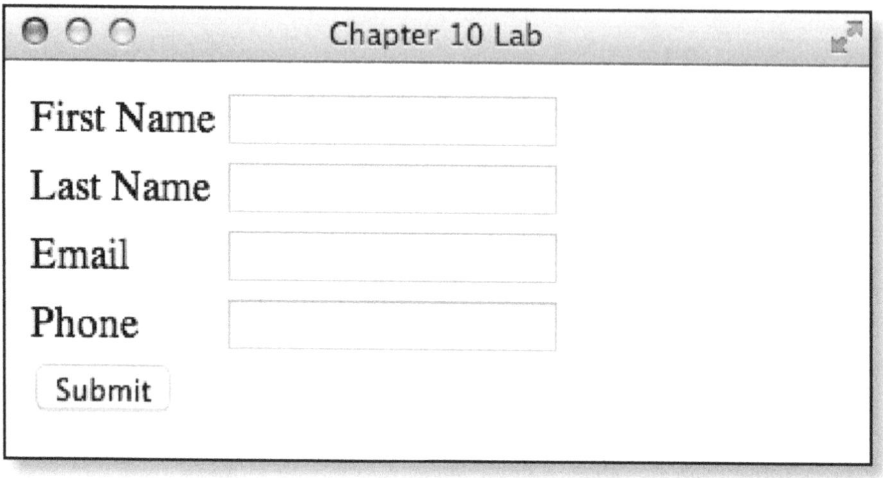

FIGURE 10 - 17

3) Each textbox must accept inputs but must also display the following texts or highlights:

- Display "**Response too short**" when the user types in information less than 3 characters long.
- Display "**Required field**" and fill the text field with red color when the user clicks in the text field but does not enter any data.

Here is the Lab Exercise Solution Starter to help you out:

CODE LISTING: LAB EXERCISE SOLUTION STARTER

```
<!DOCTYPE html>

<html>
<script language="javascript" type="text/
javascript">
function validFirst()
{

}
function validLast()
{

}
function validEmail()
{

}
function validPhone()
{

}
</script>
<head>
    <title>Chapter 10 Lab</title>
</head>
<body>
    <table>
            <tr>
                <td>First Name</td>
                <td><input type="text"
id="first" onchange="validFirst()"></td>
                <td><span id="firstError"></
td>
```

```html
        </tr>
        <tr>
            <td>Last Name</td>
            <td><input type="text"
id="last" onchange="validLast()"></td>
            <td><span id="lastError"></
td>
        </tr>
        <tr>
            <td>Email</td>
            <td><input type="text"
id="email" onchange="validEmail()"></td>
            <td><span
id="emailError"></td>
        </tr>
        <tr>
            <td>Phone</td>
            <td><input type="text"
id="phone" onchange="validPhone()"></td>
            <td><span
id="phoneError"></td>
        </tr>
        <tr>
            <td><input type="submit"
value="Submit"/></td>
            <td></td>
            <td></td>
</body>
</html>
```

4) Run the code. The output should look like this:

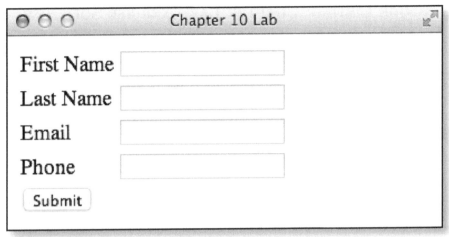

FIGURE 10 - 18

5) Complete the function codes to make the program work as described in number 3.

Make sure the program carries out the routine so that when values are entered, the appropriate message and highlight appears. See the following image:

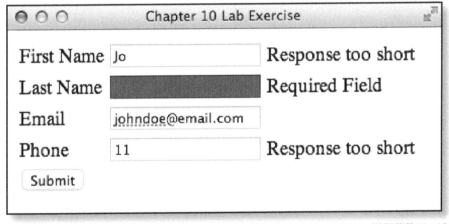

FIGURE 10 - 19

```
<!DOCTYPE html>
<html>
<script language="javascript" type="text/
javascript">
function validFirst()
{
    //alert("In validFirst()");
    var firstTextBoxContent = document.
getElementById("first").value;
    if(firstTextBoxContent != "" &&
firstTextBoxContent != null)
    {
        document.
getElementById("firstError").innerHTML= "";
        document.getElementById("first").
style.backgroundColor= "white";
        if (firstTextBoxContent.length <3)
        {
            document.
getElementById("firstError").innerHTML=
"Response too short";
        }
    } else
    {
        document.
getElementById("firstError").innerHTML=
"Required Field"
        document.getElementById("first").
style.backgroundColor= "red";
    }

}
function validLast()
{
```

```
    var lastTextBoxContent = document.
getElementById("last").value;
    if(lastTextBoxContent != "" &&
lastTextBoxContent != null)
    {
        document.
getElementById("lastError").innerHTML= "";
        document.getElementById("last").
style.backgroundColor= "white";
        if (lastTextBoxContent.length <3)
        {
            document.
getElementById("lastError").innerHTML=
"Response too short";
        }
    } else
    {
        document.
getElementById("lastError").innerHTML=
"Required Field"
        document.getElementById("last").
style.backgroundColor= "red";
    }

}
function validEmail()
{
    var emailTextBoxContent = document.
getElementById("email").value;
    if(emailTextBoxContent != "" &&
emailTextBoxContent != null)
    {
        document.
getElementById("emailError").innerHTML= "";
        document.getElementById("email").
style.backgroundColor= "white";
        if (emailTextBoxContent.length <3)
```

```javascript
        {
            document.
getElementById("emailError").innerHTML=
"Response too short";
        }
    } else
    {
        document.
getElementById("emailError").innerHTML=
"Required Field"
        document.getElementById("email").
style.backgroundColor= "red";
    }
}
function validPhone()
{
    var phoneTextBoxContent = document.
getElementById("phone").value;
    if(phoneTextBoxContent != "" &&
phoneTextBoxContent != null)
    {
        document.
getElementById("phoneError").innerHTML= "";
        document.getElementById("phone").
style.backgroundColor= "white";
        if (phoneTextBoxContent.length <3)
        {
            document.
getElementById("phoneError").innerHTML=
"Response too short";
        }
    } else
    {
        document.
getElementById("phoneError").innerHTML=
"Required Field"
        document.getElementById("phone").
```

```
style.backgroundColor= "red";
    }
}
</script>
<head>
    <title>Chapter 10 Lab Exercise </title>
</head>
<body>
    <table>
            <tr>
                <td>First Name</td>
                <td><input type="text"
id="first" onblur="validFirst()"></td>
                <td><span id="firstError"></
td>
            </tr>
            <tr>
                <td>Last Name</td>
                <td><input type="text"
id="last" onblur="validLast()"></td>
                <td><span id="lastError"></
td>
            </tr>
            <tr>
                <td>Email</td>
                <td><input type="text"
id="email" onblur="validEmail()"></td>
                <td><span
id="emailError"></td>
            </tr>
            <tr>
                <td>Phone</td>
                <td><input type="text"
id="phone" onblur="validPhone()"></td>
                <td><span
id="phoneError"></td>
            </tr>
```

```
        <tr>
            <td><input type="submit"
value="Submit"/></td>
            <td></td>
            <td></td>
</body>
</html>
```

Now that you've completed this book, take our Javascript quiz to see how well you did. A perfect score means you did a great job and really committed your time to learning Javascript.

 FINAL QUESTIONS FOR REVIEW

1) In which HTML element do we put the Javascript?
   a) <script>   c) <scripting>
   b) <js>   d) <javascript>

2) If you want to write "Hello World!" in Javascript, what would the correct syntax be?
   a) "Hello World"
   b) ("Hello World")
   c) response.write("Hello World")
   d) document.write("Hello World");

3) Where are the correct places to insert a Javascript tag?
   a) The <body> section.
   b) In the CSS file source and main HTML document.
   c) The <head> section.
   d) Both the <head> section and the <body> sections.

4) The external Javascript file must contain the <script> tag.
   a) True.
   b) False.

5) What is the correct syntax for referring to an external script called "addNumber.js"?
   a) <script type="text/javascript" href="addNumber.js">

b) <script type="text/javascript" name="sum.js">
c) <script type="text/javascript" src="addnumber.js">
d)<script type="text/javascript" src="addNumber.js">

6) How do you write "Hello there!" in an alert box?
a) alert("Hello there!");
b) msgBox("Hello there!");
c) alertBox="Hello there!";
d) alertBox("Hello there!");

7) How do you create a function?
a) function:myFunction()
b) function myFunction()
c) function:function
d) function=myFunction()

8) How do you call a function named "doRoutines"?
a) doRoutines()
b) call doRoutines()
c) call function=doRoutines
d) call function doRoutines;

9) How do you write the conditional statement if "i" is equal to 10 in Javascript?
a) if i=10;
b) if i=10 then
c) if 1==10 then
d) if (i==10)

10) How does a while-loop start using the loop counter variable x?
a) while (x<=10)   c) while (x<=10;x++)
b) while x=1 to 10   d) while (i<=10;x++);

11) How do you write a conditional statement for executing some code if "y" is NOT equal to 7?
a) if (y!=7)   c) if(y<>7)
b) if=! 7 then   d) if <>7

12) How do you add a comment in Javascript?
a) 'This is a comment'
b) <!--This is a comment-->
c) //This is a comment
d) "This is a comment"

13) How does a for-loop start?
a) for (i = 0; i <= 5; i++)

b) for (i <= 5; i++)
c) for (i = 0; i <= 5)
d) for i = to 5

14) What is the correct Javascript syntax to insert a comment that has more than one line?
a) //This comment has more than one line//
b) <!--This comment has more than one line-->
c) /*This comment has more than one line*/
d) */This comment has more than one line/*

15) What is the correct way to write a Javascript array?
a) var txt = new Array="tim", "kim", "jim", "lim", "vim"
b) var txt = new Array("tim", "kim", "jim", "lim","vim")
c) var txt = new Array:1 =("tim")2 =("kim")3 =("jim")4=("vim")
d) var txt = new Array(1: "tim",2: "kim",3: "jim" 4: "lim"5: "vim")

16) How do you round the number 7.75 to the nearest integer?
a) round(7.75)   c) Math.round(7.75)
b) rnd(7.75)   d) Math.md(7.75)

17) How can you find a client's browser name?
a) client.navName
b) navigator.appName
c) browser.name
d) window.browserName

18) How do you put a message in the browser's status bar?
a) status("put your message here")
b) window.status("put your message here")
c) statusbar = "put your message here"
d) window.status = "put your message here"

19) What would the correct Javascript syntax be if we wanted to open a new window called "xyz" which contains the URL www.learntoprogram.tv?
a) xyz=window.new("www.learntoprogram.tv");
b) xyz=window.open("www.learntoprogram.tv");
c) xyz=window.new.open("www.learntoprogram.tv");
d) xyz=window.openNew("www.learntoprogram.tv");

20) What do you call the add-on utility in Firefox that can show you what is actually happening to the codes behind the scenes?
a) Litter Bag.   c) Firefox.
b) Firebug.   d) Firetruck.

ANSWER KEY: JAVASCRIPT FOR BEGINNERS

Chapter 1.1 Introducing the Course

1. Is Javascript run on Client side or Server side?
    Answer: b. Client side

2. Javascript is defined as:
    Answer: c. A scripting language used to add interactivity to web pages

Chapter 1.2 Hello World in Javascript

1. What two items do you need to begin programming in Javascript?
    Answer: d. A web browser and a text editor.

2. What command in Javascript outputs text to the browser?
    Answer: b. document.write

3. What tag do you use within the Javascript command to separate lines in the browser?
    Answer: a.

Chapter 1.3 Where to Put Javascript

1. What's the best Javascript component to put into the head of your document?
    Answer: c. A function

2. When Ifyou wanted to create a Javascript function called sayGo, what would you have to put into the code?
    Answer: a. function sayGo()

3. What attribute do you use to load an external Javascript file?
    Answer: a src=***.js

4. Which of the following is not a place you can put Javascript?
    Answer: d. foot of the document

Chapter 2.1 Learning to Use Variables

1. In Javascript, what statement do you use to declare a variable??
>   Answer: c. var

2. What happens if you don't put quotes around a variable's text assigned vaue?
>   Answer: c. The script does not output the value.

3. What is known as the assignment operator in Javascript?
>   Answer: b. The = sign

4. Which one is a combined initialization/declation?
>   Answer: d. var Size = 0;

5. Why is it important to use the var statement everytime?
>   Answer: a. You will have trouble with variable scope if you don't.

Chapter 2.2 Variable Operators

1. What does the "+" symbol mean when you place it next to a variable?
>   Answer: a. Add the values together

2. What does the "+" symbol mean when you place it between two strings values?
>   Answer: c. Concatenate the values

3. What does the % operator do?
>   Answer: b. Gives you the remainder after division.

4. Which is the increment operator?
>   Answer: c. ++

5. How does a prefix increment operator function?
>   Answer: d. The increment takes place and then the rest of the expression is evaluated.

Chapter 3.1 Simple Conditionals

1. What would be a good definition of a conditional statement?
>   Answer: b. A statement that make sthe program branch based on a condition.

2. What does the comparison operator ">=" mean?
>   Answer: b. Greater than or equal to

3. What does the comparison operator "!=" mean?
>   Answer: a. Not equal to

4. What comparison operator would you use to create a compound statement which will logically "AND" two statements?
>   Answer: d. &&

Chapter 3.2 If-Else-If Statements

1. What does an else statement do?
>   Answer: c. Execute the next statement if the original conditional statement is false.

2. If you create an if-else-if statement, what happens when the conditional statement is true?
>   Answer: c. The program stopd evaluating other conditionals and moves on

3. Using variable *studentgrade,* how would you write a statment that tells us a student with a grade higher than 59 passes and those with a grade of 59 or lower fails?
>   Answer: c. if (studentgrade>=59) {document.write ("You passed");
>   }
>   else {document.write ("You failed"); }

Chapter 3.3 Switch-Case-Break Statements

1. What is a good definition of what a switch statement does?
>   Answer: b. Tests one condition case to see if it is true, else it seeks other conditions down the series until it encounters the default case.

2. What does the default case do?
>   Answer: c. Runs when nothing matches.

3. What happens if you forget a break statement after a case?
>   Answer: d. The program executes the other cases until a break is reached.

Chapter 4.1 Three Types of Dialog Boxes

1. What does the alert box do?
    Answer: b. Sends a message in the browser that requires a response from the user.

2. Which dialog box gives the users the ability to respond by clicking the "okay" or "cancel" button?
    Answer: b. Confirm

3. What box allows the user to enter data?
    Answer: d. Prompt

Chapter 5.1 While-Loops and Do-While-Loops

1. How does the while-loop function?
    Answer: a. Loops while a certain condition is "TRUE".

2. What loop do you use if you want to guarantee the loop will iterate at leat once before it tests the condition?
    Answer: b. Do-while loop.

3. How does a do-while loop differ from a while-loop?
    Answer: b. The condition is set at the end.

Chapter 5.2 For-Loops and Practical Application of a Loop

1. What is the first part of a for-loop?
    Answer: d. The initialization

Chapter 6.1 Function Introduction

1. What are the two parts of a function?
    Answer: c. A function call and a function definition

2. How do you declare a function?
    Answer: a. "function" followed by the name of the function

Chapter 6.2 Functions, Parameters and Returns

1. How do you pass the value of a function?

Answer: a. Put it in parentheses at the function call

2. How do you return a value to a function call?
    Answer: a return()

3. What is needed to hold the value of the return command?
    Answer: d. A variable

Chapter 6.3 Calling functions from Events

1. How do you call a function from a user-generated event?
    Answer: a. Create a button and have the button call the function
    when it is clicked.

2. What does the **onload** function do?
    Answer: c. Calls the function when the page loads.

3. What is the difference between the function events **on mousehover**
and **onclick**?
    Answer: b. **onmousehover** triggers an event when web element is
    hovered on, while **onclick** triggers the event when clicked.

Chapter 7.1 Declaring Arrays
1. What are arrays?
    Answer: a. Variables that can hold more than one value at a time.

2. What do you call the process of creating an array?
    Answer: d. Instantiation of an array.

3. In the condensed array method, where do you write the assigned
values?
    Answer: b. On the same line as the array.

4. How do you access all the members of an array?
    Answer: c. By using a loop.

Final Chapter Quiz

1) In which HTML element do we put the Javascript?
    Answer: a) <script>

2) If you want to write "Hello World!" in Javascript, what would the

correct syntax be?

   Answer: d) document.write("Hello World");

3) Where are the correct places to insert a Javascript tag?

   Answer: d) Both the <head> section and the <body> sections.

4) The external Javascript file must contain the<script> tag.

   Answer: b) False.

5) What is the correct syntax for referring to an external script called "addNumber.js"?

   Answer: d)<script type="text/javascript" src="addNumber.js">

6) How do you write "Hello there!" in an alert box?

   Answer: a) alert("Hello there!");

7) How do you create a function?

   Answer: b) function myFunction()

8) How do you call a function named "doRoutines"?

   Answer: a) doRoutines()

9) How do you write the conditional statement if "i" is equal to 10 in Javascript?

   Answer: d) if (i==10)

10) How does a while-loop start using the loop counter variable x?

   Answer: a) while (x<=10)

11) How do you write a conditional statement for executing some code if "y" is NOT equal to 7?

   Answer: a) if (y!=7)

12) How do you add a comment in Javascript?

   Answer: c) //This is a comment

13) How does a for-loop start?

   Answer: a) for (i = 0; i <= 5; i++)

14) What is the correct Javascript syntax to insert a comment that has more than one line?

   Answer: c) /*This comment has more than one line*/

15) What is the correct way to write a Javascript array?

   Answer: b) var txt = new Array("tim","kim","jim", "lim", "vim")

16) How do you round the number 7.75 to the nearest integer?

      Answer: c) Math.round(7.75)

17) How can you find a client's browser name?

      Answer: b) navigator.appName

18) How do you put a message in the browser's status bar?

      Answer: d) window.status = "put your message here"

19) What would the correct Javascript syntax be if we wanted to open a new window called "xyz" which contains the URL www.learntoprogram. tv?

      b) xyz=window.open("www.learntoprogram.tv");

20) What do you call the add-on utility in Firefox that can show you what is actually happening to the codes behind the scene?

      Answer: b) Firebug.

APPENDIX A:
SUMMARY OF COMMANDS AND FUNCTIONS TABLE

Command/Function Listed by Category	Description
HTML tags:	
<html> </html>	HTML root tag
<head> </head>	used to indicate that the tag pertains to the head of the HTML page
<title> </title>	used to contain the title of the document and found within the head
<body> </body>	used to indicate that the tag pertains to the body of the document
<script> </script>	used to set the script language to Javascript and assign the attribute type to "text/javascript"
 	break tag; used to create a break between two lines
src	source attribute link that indicates where the external Javascript source file is located
CSS:	
<ul> </ul>	used to tag unordered list
<li> </li>	used to tag list item
<em></em>	used to display text in italics
<strong></strong>	CSS style tag which renders the enclosed text bold
Comments:	
//	One-line comment
/* */	Two-line comment
Output:	

Command/Function Listed by Category	Description
document.write()	Output to screen command; displays the specified text on the web page (voided)
document.write(*userName*)	Output to screen command; displays the content of the variable *username*
document.write("John Doe")	Displays the actual content or string 'John Doe' on screen
Function:	
function *functionName*()	The syntax to name a function; *functionName* represents the name for your function; () contains the parameter(s) and may or may not have content inside the parenthesis
Variables:	
var *variableName;*	declaring a variable
var *variableName*=" ";	assigning value to a variable called *variableName*
integer value	numeric data type that has no fractional part
floating point value	numeric data type that has decimal value
Variable operators:	
string concatenation operator	(+) joins two strings or values
addition operator	(+) adds two numeric values
subtraction operator	(-) subtracts the value of the value or variable to the right side of the operator from the value to the left side of the operator
multiplication operator	(*) multiplies the values of the variable

Command/Function Listed by Category	Description
division operator	(/) divides the value of the variable assigned as the dividend in the expression by the value of the variable assigned as the divisor
modulus operator	(%) displays the remainder or fractional part resulting from a division
increment operator	adds one to the value of the assigned variable
decrement operator	subtracts one from the value of the variable
postfix operator	operator is placed after the variable
assignment operator	(=) assigns the text/value to the right of the operator to the variable on the left side of the operator
Comparison operators:	
= =	equal to; tests if both values on each side of the operator are equal
= = =	equal to value and type; tests if the values on each side of the operator are the same value and of the same data type
>	greater than; tests if the value to the left side of the operator is greater than the value to the right side of the operator
<	less than; tests if the value to the left side of the operator is less than the value to the right side of the operator
>=	greater than or equal to; tests if the value to the left side of the operator is greater than or equal to the value on the right side of the operator

Command/Function Listed by Category	Description
<=	less than; tests if the value to the left side of the operator is less than or equal to the value to the right side of the operator
!=	not equal to; tests if the values on both sides of the operator are not equal
Boolean operators:	
&&	logical AND; tests whether the conditions/expressions on both sides of the AND operator are both TRUE; if yes, the whole statement is also TRUE
||	logical OR; tests whether at least one of the conditions/expressions on either side of the OR operator is TRUE; if yes, the whole statement is TRUE
Conditionals:	
If	If the conditions/expressions are TRUE, then the codes/program routine below the if statement are run/executed, otherwise, they are not executed
If-Else	If the conditions/expressions are TRUE, then the codes/program routine below the if statement are run/executed, otherwise it executes the other code/program routine
If-Else-If	If the conditions/expressions are TRUE, then the codes/program routine below the if statement are run/executed, otherwise it executes the rest of the other code/program routines until it finds a condition that satisfies
Switch-Case-Break	Conditional that uses a 'switch' to test multiple conditions and is a quicker way to test conditional statements
Dialog Boxes:	

Command/Function Listed by Category	Description
Alert Box	a dialog box message window that shows the value assigned to the variable assigned within the *alert* command
alert (" ");	syntax for *alert* command
Confirm Box	a dialog box that asks the user a question and then the user responds by clicking 'OK' or 'Cancel'
confirm (" ")	syntax for *confirm* command
Prompt Box	a dialog box that prompts the user to type in or input data; data input is considered as string data; input numbers must be parsed to be treated as numeric data
prompt (" ")	syntax for *prompt* command
Loops	
While-loop	a conditional statement that repeats the execution of some codes after it has evaluated that the condition is TRUE
while(variableName, condition, testValue)	syntax for *while*-loop
Do-while loop	a conditional similar to while-loop that follows a different structure/syntax
do {code routine;} while condition;	syntax for do-while loop
For-loop	a compact form of conditional loops which allows programmers to set the variable, the condition, and the counter within the loop.
for (var *variableName*; *variableName*; *variableProcessing*)	syntax for *for*-loop
Parsing and rounding numbers:	

Command/Function Listed by Category	Description
parseFloat()	parses the number input as a decimal number or a fractional number
parseInt()	parses the number input as an integer number
Math.round()	rounds off numeric values accordingly
Calling functions:	
function declaration	defining the function
function call	the instance where the function is directed to run or be executed
function *functionName*()	syntax for *function*
Events:	
onclick =" "	executes a Javascript function when the button is clicked
onload= " "	executes a function once the page has loaded
onmouseover= " "	executes a function when the mouse pointer hovers over an HTML element in the browser
onunload= " "	executes a function when the user exits a page
Declaring Arrays:	
standard method:	
var *firstNames*=new Array();	syntax for declaring an array through standard method
firstNames= "John";	example of instantiating an array element
condensed method:	
var *arrayName* = new Array ("dog", "cat", "mouse")	syntax and example of assigning values to an array using condensed method

Command/Function Listed by Category	Description
literal array method:	
var *arrayName* = ["Apple", "Google", Cnet"]	syntax and example of assigning arrays using literal array method
document. write(*arrayNameI*.length);	command and syntax for displaying the length of an array
arrayName.push(*new iteration value 1, new iteration value 2, ...);*	function that adds a new element to the array
arrayName.pop(new array element 1, new array element 2, ...);	function that removes the last element of the array, in this example, array element 2
arrayName.sort();	syntax for sorting an array; sort arranges the members of the array alphabetically
arrayName.splice(index number of first item to be removed, number of objects to be removed);	syntax for splicing an array; splice allows removal of objects or array members anywhere within the array
Objects, Properties and Methods:	
objectName.propertyName	syntax for defining property attributes
charAt()	displays the character at its index position in the string
charCodeAt()	displays the Unicode value for each of the string characters
indexOf()	used to find the first occurrence of a character in the series
replace()	used to replace a selected set of strings with a set of different string values
split()	used to convert a string separated by commas into an array
appCodename	discloses the browser's codename used

Command/Function Listed by Category	Description
appcode	identifies the name of the browser used
appVersion	reports the current version of the browser used
innerWidth	tells the browser's inner width (in pixels)
innerHeight	tells the inner height of the browser (in pixels)
location	tells the location where the webpage or document is stored or located
protocol	extended property of *location* indicating the webpage's protocol used (http, https or file)
Screen Object:	
screen.height	tells the height of the actual monitor used
screen.colorDepth	tells the color resolution of the user's computer display unit
Document Object & InnerHTML properties:	
document object	refers to all elements found within an HTML page document
getElementById().value	command and syntax to extract entries from text box elements
innerHTML property	refers to webpage content and the ability to change these contents within the page dynamically
Firebug	Add-on utility in Firefox that can show you what is actually happening to the codes behind the scenes.

The Development Club

https://learntoprogram.tv/course/ultimate-monthly-bundle/?src=BOOKAD

This comprehensive membership includes:

• Access to EVERY course in LearnToProgram's growing library--including our exciting lineup of new courses planned for the coming year. This alone is over a $2,500 value.

• Access to our Live Courses. Take any of our online instructor-led courses which normally cost up to $300. These courses will help you advance your professional skills and learn important techniques in web, mobile, and game development.

• Free certification exams. As you complete your courses, earn LearnToProgram's certifications by passing optional exams. All certification fees are waived for club members.

• Weekly instructor hangouts where you can ask questions about course material, your personal learning goals, or just chat!

• Free Personal Learning Plans. You'll never wonder what you should take next to achieve your goals!

• The LearnToProgram guarantee!

THE LEARNTOPROGRAM GUARANTEE

Our Guarantee:
If you watch the course videos and complete the lab exercises, **you will learn to program.** Guaranteed. If you don't, we will personally pay your membership fees for the next 90 days.

The Development Club

Use Coupon Code: BOOK19
and get $20 off your first month!

More Information at
https://**LearnToProgram.tv**

19.99

CPSIA information can be obtained at www.ICGtesting.com
Printed in the USA
LVOW04s2130101014

408315LV00008B/79/P